# WORLD WAR II
## RICHMOND
## VIRGINIA

WALTER S. GRIGGS JR.

Charleston — London

THE
History
PRESS

Published by The History Press
Charleston, SC 29403
www.historypress.net

Cover image courtesy of the *Richmond Times-Dispatch* Collection, Valentine Richmond History Center.

First published 2013

Manufactured in the United States

ISBN 978.1.62619.026.9

Library of Congress CIP data applied for.

*This book is dedicated to my wife, Frances Pitchford Griggs,
and to my daughter, Cara Frances Griggs.*

*Thou salt not kill.*
*—Exodus 20:12*

*It is well that war is so terrible* [otherwise] *we would be too fond of it.*
*—General Robert Edward Lee*

*War justifies everything.*
*—Napoleon*

*I love war and responsibility and excitement.*
*—General George S. Patton Jr.*

*I have seen enough of* [war] *to make me look upon it as the sum of all evils.*
*—Lieutenant General Thomas J. "Stonewall" Jackson*

*War is hell!*
*—General William T. Sherman*

*I hate war.*
*—President Franklin D. Roosevelt*

*War is always a matter of doing evil in the hope that some good may come of it.*
*—Captain Sir Basil Liddell Hart*

*I hope to God that I have fought my last battle.*
*—The Duke of Wellington*

*Mankind has grown strong in eternal struggles and it will only perish through eternal peace.*
*—Adolf Hitler*

*Believe! Obey! Fight!*
*—Benito Mussolini*

*When I died they washed me out of the turret with a hose.*
*—Randall Jarred, "The Death of the Ball Turret Gunner"*

*Another improvement that we made…was that we built our gas chambers to*
*accommodate two hundred people at one time.*
*—Rudolph Hess*

*We are getting killed on the beaches—let's go inshore and get killed.*
*—U.S. soldier, Omaha Beach*

*Before we're through with them, the Japanese language will be spoken only in hell.*
*—Admiral William F. Halsey*

*Cease firing, but if any enemy planes appear, shoot them down in a friendly fashion.*
*—Admiral William F. Halsey*

*Should we continue to fight…it would lead to the total extinction of*
*human civilization.*
*—Emperor Hirohito of Japan*

*For your tomorrow*
*We gave our today.*
*—British War Memorial*

*When we moderns go to war, we start a forest fire that stops at nothing, spares*
*nobody, and destroys everything.*
*—Harry Emerson Fosdick*

# CONTENTS

# PREFACE

World War II was the defining event in the lives of those who lived through the days when the "lights went out all over the world." Although we still remember the great battles and leaders, we have largely forgotten the sacrifices of those who fought the war on the homefront. But victory could not have been achieved without the contributions of the men and women who stayed at home and collected junk, stepped on tin cans, wore cuff-less pants, built airplanes and tanks, stood on buildings watching for enemy planes and felt the incomprehensible loss of loved ones. This book is my effort to record many of the important daily events of the Richmonders who lived through those days so that their contributions to the war effort will not be forgotten.

On a personal note, I was born a year before Pearl Harbor and have few memories of the war. However, when I started reading the old newspapers, I came to understand how much I owe to my parents, Dorothy and Walter Griggs. They endured years filled with anxiety but never really told me about their own experiences. I am also grateful to my brother, Bob, who was born after the war but provided me with many helpful insights. During and after the war, my grandparents Martin and Maggie Feitig lived with us. Long after the war, I saw my grandfather resharpen his own razor blades and make jars of apple sauce last longer by putting water into the jar. After doing the research for this book, I understand his somewhat bizarre behavior. What he learned to do to save blades and food became a part of his life.

I also want to express my gratitude to the following people, libraries and archives: the Richmond Public Library, St. John's United Church of Christ and the reference archivists at the Library of Virginia and Tom Silvestri and Heather Moon of the *Richmond Times-Dispatch*. Of special note is the help of David Grabarek of the Library of Virginia, who taught me how to use a computer mouse to "hover" over a computer icon.

My Ginter Park Elementary School Class of 1953 shared many of their childhood memories and memorabilia with me. I would like to express my appreciation to all of my classmates, especially Ruth Decker Caudill, Clint Rose, Carolyn Whitworth Brittain, Judith Reynolds Johnson and Jean Bear.

Several people gave me the benefits of their own research and memories, including Susan Guckenberg, Sanford Williamson and Joan Beck Willis. I want to thank Betty Hach Lohmann for letting me use the prayer she prayed at Highland Park Elementary School on D-Day. I also want to express my appreciation to Carolyn Whitworth Brittain and Judith Reynolds Johnson for allowing me to use material from their World War II collections. I have greatly benefited from the encouragement and support of a number of people, including Jill Kramer, Linda Pontius, Susan Griggs, Dr. Jerome Becker, Dr. Ann Williams, Dr. Marianne Miller and Dr. Glenn Gilbreath.

On issues of race, I have spent many hours talking with my academic colleague Dr. Annie Stith-Willis. Her insights have been invaluable to me, as has her friendship. Also very helpful were conversations with my former student Jay "C" Paul, who taught me a lot about submarine warfare.

At The History Press, I want to thank Banks Smithers, who provided invaluable assistance in helping me prepare this book for publication; Katie Parry, who has made writing a pleasure by arranging so many book signings;    Meredith Riddick, who does a great job in sending books to various outlets; and Jamie Muehl, who prepared the manuscript for publication.

As always, my wife, Frances, spent hours trying to make this book readable by checking and editing every word that I wrote. If "Rosy the Riveter" got us through the war, "Frances the Proofer" got me through this book. Thank you, Frances!

Finally, I want to thank my daughter, Cara, who, as a reference archivist, helped me locate much material and, as a photographer, did the editing of all of the images and prepared them for publication. Thank you, Cara!

*Walter S. Griggs Jr.*
VJ Day 2013
Richmond, Virginia

# INTRODUCTION

*There's a long, long trail a-winding*
*Into the land of my dreams;*
*Where the nightingales are singing*
*And a white moon beams.*
*There's a long, long night of waiting*
*Until my dreams all come true;*
*Till the day when I'll be going down*
*That long, long trail with you.*
*—Stoddard King and Alonzo Elliott*

The Carillon in Byrd Park can be seen from many locations in Richmond. This magnificent 240-foot-tall "singing tower" is a tribute to those Virginians who died "over there" in the Great War. A bell tower was selected to honor the war dead and to call attention to the fact that when the war ended in Europe in November 1918, church bells rang in celebration.

At its dedication in 1932, more than fifteen thousand people stood in the shadow of the Carillon and heard a dedicatory prayer that expressed the hope "that the bells may ring out the thousand wars of old and ring in the thousand years of peace." Senator Alban W. Barkley of Kentucky observed, "It is a beautiful thing you have done here to erect a memorial in perpetual honor of the undying fame of those who died in the war." As part of the ceremony, the bells of the Carillon rang out "Lead, Kindly Light," "Onward, Christian Soldiers," "There's a Long, Long Trail A-winding" and "America."

The Carillon in Byrd Park that was dedicated to the Virginians who died in World War I.
*Photograph by Walter Griggs.*

Those people who were at the dedication had no idea that the peace they were celebrating was about to end in a modern-day Armageddon.

Two months after the dedication of this tower of peace in Richmond, Virginia, Adolf Hitler became chancellor of Germany. Richmonders who read the *Richmond News Leader* of January 30, 1933, were greeted by a front-page picture of Hitler that, by any standards, showed him as evil personified. The lead paragraph stated, "Adolf Hitler, picturesque leader of the German Fascists, was made Chancellor of Germany." An editorial in the same paper commented, "Hitler says that he will govern constitutionally, and from today's proclamations, his party has dropped its anti-Semitic slurs." The world would soon discover that it could not trust Adolf Hitler.

In rapid succession, Hitler abolished trade unions, dismantled all political parties, renewed his anti-Semitic agenda and led Germany out of the League of Nations. Richmonders heard about the "night of the Long Knives," which was a violent, bloody purge of those opposed to Hitler. With his opponents eliminated, Hitler became president of Germany, took the title of *Führer* and started to implement his program of conquest and extermination of the Jewish people.

Hitler annexed Austria in 1938 in his effort to unite all German-speaking people. The rationale was that there were six million Germans living in Austria, and they should be part of Germany. This forced annexation, known as the *Anschluss*, was the theme of the popular musical *The Sound of Music*. Although not known at the time, this was the beginning of the end of peace in Europe.

On September 30, 1938, European leaders signed the Treaty of Munich, and Hitler was given the Sudetenland of Czechoslovakia, which, like Austria, had a large German population. Hitler assured the conferees at the Munich Conference that this was the end of his land claims in Europe. Thus, Czech freedom was sacrificed for the promise of Adolf Hitler seeking no more land for Germany. Hitler believed that people would believe a big lie more than a small lie. His promise was a big lie—and for a time, people believed him.

Following his meeting with Hitler at Munich, Neville Chamberlain, prime minister of Great Britain, came home proclaiming to the cheering British people that he had achieved "peace in our time." The world would soon learn that appeasement was not a viable option, although it was the diplomatic strategy of Neville Chamberlain. This painful lesson from Munich has continued to influence foreign policy to the present day.

Having achieved his goals at Munich, Hitler started his persecution of the Jews. On the nights of the November 9 and 10, 1938, the German authorities

Cattle car like those used to transport Jews to various death camps. It is on display in front of the Virginia Holocaust Museum. *Photograph by Walter Griggs.*

stood aside as the Nazis launched their most destructive campaign against the Jews to date. Over one thousand synagogues were burned, along with other property owned by Jews. The streets were filled with broken glass from the vandalism of Jewish synagogues, shops, stores and homes. Because of all of the broken glass in the streets, this attack on the Jews is known as *Kristallnacht,* or the "night of the broken glass." The Jews of Europe were soon rounded up like cattle and shipped to concentration camps in boxcars from which millions did not return. Most Germans did not try to save their former friends and neighbors. Martin Niemöller summed up the lack of concern by writing:

> *First they came for the Socialists, and I did not speak out—Because I was not a Socialist.*
> *Then they came for the Trade Unionists, and I did not speak out—Because I was not a Trade Unionist.*

*Then they came for the Jews, and I did not speak out—Because I was not a Jew.*
*Then they came for me—and there was no one left to speak for me.*

As the Jews were being rounded up, Adolf Hitler's legions continued to goose-step across Europe. In March 1939, while the world watched and did nothing, Hitler's armies seized what remained of Czechoslovakia. Following the seizure, England and France promised to defend Poland from the scourge of the Nazi Cross. Appeasement was no longer going to be the policy. In Richmond, the Carillon still stood as a beacon of peace, but its bells were rarely rung. In Europe, however, more and more people were singing a song:

*Deutschland, Deutschland über alles,*
*Über alles in der Welt.*

And there was a new greeting in Germany and the conquered nations: *Heil Hitler!*

# CHAPTER 1

# EUROPE IN FLAMES, 1939

*We're going to hang out the washing on the Siegfried Line,*
*Have you any dirty washing, mother dear?*
*We're gonna hang out the washing on the Siegfried Line.*
*'Cause the washing day is here.*
*—Jimmy Kennedy*

Across Europe, world-changing events came in rapid succession. In late August 1939, Russia and Germany signed a nonaggression pact. Now assured that his eastern front was secure, Hitler prepared to invade Poland. Presumably for an unannounced port visit, the World War I German battleship *Schleswig-Holstein* arrived off the coast of Danzig, Poland. Hitler then faked an attack on a German outpost to make it seem as though the Poles were attacking the Germans so the Germans could justify an invasion. Then the 280mm main guns of the battleship unleashed their screaming salvos on the Poles. And the sky over Poland was filled with German aircraft, including Stukas, Messerschmitts and Heinkels, while German soldiers and powerful Panzer tanks streamed across the Polish border. To conquer Poland, Hitler employed the blitzkrieg—a rapid advance by a powerful force against an unsuspecting nation.

No longer willing to appease a tyrant, Neville Chamberlain spoke from the cabinet room at Number 10 Downing Street in London and announced that a state of war existed with Germany; there would be no peace in our time as promised. France joined in the declaration of war—appeasement was now replaced by tanks, artillery, soldiers, airplanes and ships. Hitler's insatiable appetite to gobble up other nations would now be challenged. Soon British troops were heard singing, "It's a Long Way to Tipperary," a popular song from World War I, as they marched off to France to fight for king and country.

Richmonders might not have realized it at the time, but the war in Europe would soon touch, change and then engulf them. The *Richmond Times-Dispatch* of September 1, 1939, proclaimed in banner headline, "Four Polish Cities Bombed, Fighting in Danzig Reported." One columnist fumed, "A lone megalomaniac [Hitler] has elected to plunge Europe into war. Unwilling to negotiate, except on his own terms, he determined that all who stand in his way shall be ruthlessly crushed." The German people were reportedly stunned by the invasion and the start of what would become World War II.

Many political leaders were hopefully suggesting—and many Richmonders were in agreement—that the United States should stay out of the war. But one Richmond columnist wrote, "We can't keep out of it; we're sure to get into it sooner or later." However, President Roosevelt apparently was of the same mind as many Richmonders when he affirmed that the "United States should stay out of the war...unless it [the United States] is clearly in imminent danger of attack." But subsequent events would make this an impossible objective. By the end of September 1939, Poland had been conquered, and the Nazi flag was seen flying from its buildings while its Jewish population was being exterminated.

Following Hitler's conquest of Poland, the world seemed to lapse into a period of peace from September 1939 to April 1940. Nothing seemed to happen. Had a world war been averted? This period was called the *Sitzkrieg*, or Phony War. Richmonders, like many people, soon felt there was nothing to be concerned about and no need to be alarmed. However, there were several events that reminded people that a war was going on, and they were reported in bold headlines in the Richmond newspapers. For example, Hitler's navy suffered a severe setback when the German pocket battleship *Graf Spee* was scuttled by its crew after an engagement with the British navy. This news was well received in Richmond.

Not so well received was the news that parking meters were being installed on the streets for the first time. Richmonders also learned that the State Library Building was about to be completed on Broad Street, as well as the State Highway Building. Another major addition to the skyline was the Medical College of Virginia Hospital, which was nearing completion. The hospital had a revolving aircraft-warning beacon on the top as a collision avoidance measure for low-flying airplanes. Within a few months, the beacon would be turned off to hide the hospital from enemy aircraft.

# CHAPTER 2

# THERE WILL ALWAYS BE
# AN ENGLAND, 1940

*There'll always be an England,*
*And England shall be free,*
*If England means as much to you*
*As England means to me.*
*—Ross Parker and Hughie Charles*

*The last time I saw Paris*
*Her heart was warm and gay*
*I heard the laughter of her heart*
*In every street café.*
*—Oscar Hammerstein and Jerome Kern*

On May 10, 1940, the local newspaper headlines were in large, bold type and proclaimed, "Germany Invades Holland, Belgium, and Luxemburg." The next day, Richmonders read in the newspaper that Great Britain had a new prime minister, the Nazi-hating Winston Churchill. Speaking for the first time as prime minister, Churchill warned the English people that the conquered nations would face a "long night of barbarism…unless we conquer, as conquer we must, as conquer we shall." He then ended with words that will live as long as civilization exists: "Let us therefore brace ourselves to our duties, and so bear ourselves that, if the British Empire and its Commonwealth lasts for a thousand years, men will say, 'This was their finest hour.'"

A Nazi rally during the war. *Canadian Archives.*

In the same month, Hitler unleashed the blitzkrieg on France. Outflanking the vaunted Maginot Line, Hitler's juggernaut raced through France and forced the defending French and British forces to withdraw to Dunkirk on the French Coast. The British saved their army by sending every conceivable kind of vessel across the English Channel to carry the soldiers back to England. Britain now stood alone against the forces of Nazism. The fall of France and the threat to Great Britain made the United States feverishly prepare for a war that now seemed inevitable. Even with war looming, some people did not trust the government to tell them the truth about the world situation. They felt that the United States was about to be sucked into a European war like it had been in World War I. One man wrote to the newspaper and stated that Washington needed a delousing. Richmonders heard impassioned voices lifted in protest against America's possible involvement in a European War. Organizations like America First and the German American Bund and well-known personalities like Charles Lindbergh and Father Charles Coughlin spoke out against any active involvement of the United States to support England.

Richmonders were certainly familiar with their views, but they continued to support England's fight to survive.

To meet the growing crisis, on May 30, 1940, Governor James H. Price of Virginia issued a proclamation setting up a State Defense Council to plan for what might lie ahead for Virginians. To head the council, Dr. Douglas Southall Freeman, the city's well-known author, editor and historian, was selected. Dr. Freeman lived by the principle: "Time alone is irreplaceable, waste it not."

And time was not on the side of the United States. President Roosevelt was scheduled to make a graduation speech at the University of Virginia on June 10, 1940, the same day Italy declared war on France and Great Britain. The president reworked his speech on the train from Washington to address the Italian declaration. At the commencement, he was defiant when he said, "The hand that held the dagger has stuck it into the back of its neighbor." These words signaled an end to the United States being a neutral nation. From the grounds of the University of Virginia, word went forth that the United States would provide all-out aid to the democracies and begin an unprecedented buildup of the nation's armed forces.

As the clouds of war thickened and darkened over Europe, Richmonders started to collect aluminum scrap for use in war-related industries. Soon there were 39,910 pounds of scrap in "Aluminum Park" at Broad and Robinson Streets. Then Congress authorized the mobilization of the National Guard in July 1940. About two months later, the War Department called out the fifty-five thousand officers and men of the National Guard. As expected, the first Richmond unit, the Headquarters Battery of the Fifty-fourth Field Artillery Brigade, was mobilized. The unit was headquartered in a building on Seventh Street.

With the removal of the National Guard from state service, the governor issued an executive order authorizing the creation of the Virginia Protective Force, which later became the Virginia State Guard, that would soon play an important role in protecting the homefront, as would the newly created Richmond Office of Civil Defense. Also, Richmond had a new mayor. Gordon Ambler, an attorney, assumed office on September 1, 1940. In the years ahead, he would be responsible for the city's 200,000 citizens. It soon became his responsibility to lead Richmond through uncharted territory as he prepared the city for war.

Richmonders had hoped to stay out of the war, but this hope was in conflict with world events. In September 1940, the United States got closer to war when the government gave the British fifty over-age destroyers to bolster their fleet in return for leases on some naval bases. In a newspaper story, a writer stated that this transfer was an act of war. He then observed, "But how much difference does that make under the circumstances?" One of the transferred destroyers was the USS *Fairfax*, which was renamed the HMS *Richmond* upon its arrival in England. Across the years, local citizens would send "comfort items" to the British crew, and a bond would develop between the ship and the city.

In the same month, President Roosevelt signed into law the first peacetime draft bill. The president commented, "The United States is marshaling its strength to avert the terrible fate of nations whose weaknesses invited attack." On October 16, 1940, pursuant to the new draft law, Richmonders between the ages of twenty-one and thirty-five registered for the draft at one of over forty registration places, including the basement of Binford Junior High School. In segregated Richmond, black men registered in schools assigned to black students. In some of the elementary schools, big men sat in small chairs made for first-graders and quipped, "I want to go to school, I like my pony and I like to play." One reporter wrote that "there was sort of a grim humor" among those registering. Public school teachers did most of the registering. One teacher commented that "she did not know Richmond had so many handsome young men." When the men emerged from the registration process, they carried cards that read, "Be alert. Keep in touch with your Local Board. Carry this card at all times."

While some men were registering for the draft, other young men paraded on the Boulevard with posters proclaiming, "We Want Peace, We Hate War, and You Know It!" Other Richmonders tried to avoid the draft by proving that they were not "intelligent enough to obey military commands and to be able to transport themselves by walking." Before the war ended, one out of every eight Richmond residents would wear the nation's uniform.

About the same time that men were registering for the draft, President Roosevelt, in a campaign speech in Boston, assured Americans, "Your boys are not going to be sent into any foreign war." In an effort to stay neutral and perhaps cool war fervor, Richmond Public School superintendent Jesse H. Binford ordered teachers to assume a nonpartisan attitude and to discourage discussions that might tend to inflame the pupils. This was coupled with a plea from the school board chairman, Dr. Roshier W. Miller, to teachers reminding them to teach Americanism and democracy. He wrote: "Keep the children's hearts and minds free of hate."

Unfortunately, the war brought out hate in some people. There was one case where unknown individuals defamed innocent people. The target was

Nolde Brothers Bakery, which operated in both Richmond and Norfolk. Because the family was of German origin, there was a whispering campaign that they were Nazi sympathizers. The bakery started to run ads pointing out that they had "had a record of patriotism since the business was founded in 1892." An editorial writer commented that "the Nolde family is as patriotic as the Governor of Virginia or the Mayor of Richmond." The Noldes stated that they would prosecute anyone who questioned their patriotism. The campaign faded away, and Carl William Nolde, the son of the founder of the bakery, went to war wearing the uniform of a master sergeant in the United States Army.

While the United States prepared for war, Edward R. Murrow was reporting from London, where German aircraft were dropping bombs almost nightly. He opened his radio broadcast with these words: "This is London." Standing on a rooftop, he reported to the American people that Britain was fighting for its very existence as the German Luftwaffe (air force) conducted nightly raids that did not discriminate between soldiers and civilians or between ancient cathedrals or ammunitions plants. Murrow would always end his broadcast with the phrase: "Good Night and Good Luck," which was what Londoners said to one another when they finished a conversation at night.

While some people were saying, "Good night," many British pilots remembered the song sung by Vera Lynn, "Wish Me Luck as You Wave Me Goodbye," as they climbed into the cockpits of their fighters. And soon in the skies over England, German pilots would yell, "*Achtung*, Spitfires!" as courage met courage and planes started twisting and turning as they fell in flames from the sky.

Before the end of 1940, Hitler's Luftwaffe had been defeated by the British pilots in their Spitfires and Hurricane fighters, and it was of these pilots that Winston Churchill said, "Never in the field of human conflict was so much owed by so many to so few." Richmonders followed the course of the Battle of Britain in their daily newspapers and on the radio, especially since some of the Battle of Britain pilots were from the United States.

As 1940 drew to a close, the Richmond newspapers editorialized, "Can anyone, who studies recent European history with his eyes open, doubt that the Nazis are out to conquer and enslave Europe, and then to attack us, either by economic or military and naval means or both?" The year ended with a lot of Christmas shopping, perhaps as a retreat from reality, but one could not always ignore reality when the world was in flames.

CHAPTER 3

# REMEMBER PEARL HARBOR, 1941

*Let's Remember Pearl Harbor.*
*As we go to meet the foe—*
*Let's Remember Pearl Harbor*
*As we did the Alamo.*
*—Don Reid*

With more and more military activity in Norfolk and Camp Lee, many servicemen came to Richmond on weekends to find recreation and entertainment. The social activities were coordinated by the Richmond Defense Unit of the State Defense Council. It also became necessary to find places for visitors to stay, so three Richmond armories were opened to provide facilities for visiting servicemen. The Grays and Blues Armories were used for white men, and the Howitzer's Armory was used for black men. For thirty-five cents, a serviceman obtained lodging, sheets, towels, soap and showers.

Some of the other organizations that provided for the needs of the soldiers were the YMCA, the Red Cross and the Jewish Army-Navy Group that opened in the basement of Temple Beth Ahabah. Also, downtown churches, including St. Paul's Episcopal, Centenary Methodist and Seventh Street Christian, welcomed soldiers. The Army Mom's Club and the Navy Mother's Club maintained facilities for visiting soldiers and sailors. At all of these facilities, sewing and mending services were available, along with religious material. To further support the servicemen, the USO (United

Service Organization) sent representatives to Richmond to take steps to incorporate the city into its programs. In December, the USO took over the major burden of seeing to the welfare of the soldiers, although other organizations continued to operate.

In March 1941, Lend Lease became law, making the United States the "Arsenal of Democracy" since it could now provide military supplies to those nations fighting the Axis powers. And in that same month, President Roosevelt proclaimed that an unlimited national emergency confronted this nation. The gathering clouds of war turned several shades darker.

The war in Europe moved to the high seas when the German battleship *Bismarck* sank the British ship HMS *Hood*. The British navy then sank the *Bismarck*. Most Richmonders were quite happy with the death of this German ship that had terrorized shipping in the Atlantic Ocean. There were even efforts to show how the United States helped in sinking the ship. An editorial commented, "The fact that American-made planes took leading roles in shadowing the German ship is symbolic of the ever-mounting aid which Britain is receiving from this country."

Germany invaded Russia in June 1941, which was a terrible blunder. Like Napoleon before him, Hitler did not take into account that the Russian winter was a formidable ally for the Soviet nation, as was the determination of the people to defend Mother Russia regardless of the cost. Before the invasion ended, burned-out Panzer tanks were scattered across the landscape, and many Germans froze to death. These soldiers would never see the *Vaterland* (Fatherland) again.

While Richmonders were much more interested in the war in Europe, Japan was on the move in the east. As part of its expansion plans in 1936, Japan joined Germany in a treaty to provide a two-front threat to the Soviet Union; however, Japan was not interested in getting into the European war. Instead, Japan attacked China in 1937 and inflicted incomprehensible cruelty on the Chinese people. Phrases like the "Rape of Nanking" entered the vocabulary. Later in the year, the Japanese attacked the USS *Panay*, which was flying the United States' flag. The ship was sunk. Japan apologized for the incident and paid damages. But many Richmonders did not believe that it was a mistake. This sinking could have been used as a provocation for war, but it was not. However, the tide of public opinion in the United States was clearly against the Japanese, although little mention was made in the local newspapers of Japanese aggression compared to the European conflict. In August 1941, the United States, which supplied 80 percent of Japanese oil imports, declared a complete oil embargo. Without oil, Japan's economy

WRONG

The Bismarck was scuttle by the Germans

would soon be in ruins, and it would not be able to maintain and strengthen its military. Japan had to take some action. Not known to the United States was the fact that Japanese students had been using an attack on Pearl Harbor, Hawaii, as an academic exercise for many years.

While problems were building with Japan, the conflict with Germany escalated. On May 21, 1941, the freighter SS *Robin Moor*, flying the United States' flag, was sunk in the South Atlantic by German U-boat *69*. As a result of this sinking, the United States State Department required Germany and Italy to close all of their consulates in the United States, except for their embassies. In retaliation, Germany took the same action against the United States. Germany did not pay the United States the demanded reparations for the *Robin Moor*. The loss of the ship started a "shooting war" on the high seas, which was a war in fact but not in name.

Richmond's newspapers continued to carry war news on a daily basis, and some people were already growing tired of it even though they were not fighting the war. There were also comments that it was a "terrible thing to witness the war psychology which was now spreading so rapidly." While Richmonders were complaining about the emphasis on the war, Churchill and Roosevelt were drafting the Atlantic Charter, which would determine policies on war and peace.

On September 4, 1941, the American destroyer USS *Greer* was in the North Atlantic, flying the American flag, when it was attacked by German U-boat *652*. The U-boat fired on the *Greer* with torpedoes, but there were no hits. Germany claimed that the *Greer* had first opened fire on the U-boat. The United States insisted that the Germans fired first before the *Greer* dropped its depth charges. An editorial in the city's newspapers commented, "Why did a German submarine fire torpedoes at the United States destroyer *Greer* in broad daylight?" Of interest to the city was that one Richmonder was on board the *Greer* when it was attacked and that the ship had been used as a training ship by Richmond naval reservists in 1936.

This was the first incident in which a United States naval ship was fired on by a German vessel. President Roosevelt used the attack to announce that "from now on, if German or Italian vessels of war enter waters, the protection of which is necessary for American defense, they do so at their own peril." The undeclared war was getting more intense. How much longer would the guns remain silent?

Another reminder of the military's preparation occurred on September 5, 1941, when a convoy of over two thousand trucks rolled through Richmond without advance notice. The convoy carried members of the

Second Army Corps going from the Carolinas, where they had been training, to their New England bases. Some of the northern soldiers yelled from their trucks, "You rebels are OK with us!" The convoy created a daylong traffic problem for impatient citizens, but this was not the end of the convoys. Motorists were warned that more convoys were on the way. United States Highway 1 through Richmond was a vital north–south route and was a frequent convoy route.

As the convoys rolled through Richmond, it was reported that an American-owned ship, the SS *Steel Seafarer*, was sunk by an attacking airplane in the Red Sea. These and other recent sinkings were confirmation of the Nazis' notice that they would sink any ship in a war area "regardless of nationality." The situation only got worse when the USS *Kearney*, a United States destroyer, was fired on by the Germans. Eleven Americans died, but the ship was able to return to port. Some lawmakers suggested that this aggression by the Germans was designed to draw Japan into an attack in the Pacific. Relations between the United States, Germany and Japan were at the breaking point—perhaps beyond the breaking point.

In early November, Richmonders opened their newspapers to see the following bold headline: "Torpedo Sinks U.S. Destroyer." The USS *Reuben James* was sunk by a U-boat while on convoy duty west of Iceland. Now, President Roosevelt ordered the navy to "shoot on sight" any Axis warships encountered. Once again, there was ample provocation to start a war, but war was not declared. It was as if Hitler was seeing how much the American nation would tolerate before it would fight. He would soon find out.

In mid-November, Virginia celebrated Civilian Defense Week. The theme was "a nation founded upon the essential freedoms must defend them." In many local churches, the clergy dwelt on "the freedoms Americans enjoy." It was also reported that defense service units in Richmond and other Virginia communities were being organized. People who volunteered were given training in home nursing, nutrition, recreation and other defense activities. The plan also called for the establishment, as needed, of committees on safety, which would manage police, fire, disaster, air-raid shelters, transportation, motor corps, postwar activities and finance.

Every day Richmonders were exposed to more war news in headlines, in magazines, in movie newsreels or on the radio. The radio was the way many people kept up with the fast-changing world events. Radio newsmen had their own unique way of opening their broadcasts. Walter Winchell would say, "Good evening, Mr. and Mrs. North and South America and all the ships at sea, let's go to press." Lowell Thomas would open his broadcast by

The radio used by Frances Pitchford's family to listen to the latest news of the war. *Frances Pitchford Griggs Collection.*

saying, "Good evening, everybody." And he would close with the phrase, "So long until tomorrow." Other well-known newsmen were Elmer Davis, Drew Pearson and Robert Trout. ✛ *H. V. Kaltenborne*

In November, the first draftees from Richmond under the Selective Service Act were inducted into the armed forces in a ceremony at the Blues Armory. Then a medical service unit was organized in Richmond and throughout Virginia. In case of war, these units would be asked "to make provisions for evacuation, clearance hospitals, ambulance units, casualty stations, first-aid posts, and decontamination stations."

On a lighter note, the *Richmond Times-Dispatch* reported that three soldiers were seeking Richmond girls with whom to correspond. Two of the soldiers were American, and one was English. The reporter commented, "The

Americans, finicky as usual, specify girls between eighteen and twenty-five. The Englishman says, just girls." The lovesick soldiers were stationed in Hawaii, and their address was Schofield Barracks. Within two weeks, these barracks would be attacked by the Japanese.

Obviously, there were plenty of girls in Richmond, since more than 250 of them, "who have been whirling about in the arms of stalwart soldiers at the Defense Service Unit dances, would get their service pins." The ceremony was held at the Mosque (now the Richmond Landmark Theater). Each pin had the seal of the City of Richmond and the words "Richmond Defense Unit" on it. The soldier escorts attached the pins to the dresses of the girls being recognized. In these days of racial segregation, a similar event was held for the black girls at the Howitzer's Armory in recognition of their attendance at dances, and the mayor of Richmond presided at both ceremonies. Before peace returned, more than 12,000 girls and 2,500 chaperones would entertain soldiers in Richmond and the surrounding camps.

If needed, young women who attended the dances were also able to get advice on dating. Betty Bly, a popular columnist, gave advice to the lovelorn in the *Richmond Times-Dispatch*. The following letter was typical:

> *Dear Miss Bly:*
> *I am very much in love with Bill. But he just told me that he would have a date with another girl every night beginning December 24 to December 31. Do you think if he loved me he could stay away from me one whole week and devote his time entirely to someone else? I also like another boy that I do not see very much. What should I do?*
> */s/ Unhappy*

> *Dear Unhappy:*
> *Play off the second boy against Bill. See if you can arrange to have a date every night during Christmas week and make sure Bill hears about it.*
> */s/ Betty Bly*

As Christmas approached, shoppers flocked to Broad Street. Lionel Electric trains were a popular purchase at $6.00, and reversible topcoats sold for $10.98. Nolde Brothers Bakery was selling what was described as "the most tempting gift of all—fruit cakes." Stores like Dabney and Bugg were selling draperies, Safeway was selling Jell-Well dessert and pudding and a popular detergent was Super Suds, which claimed to provide "Less Sneezy Dust than other leading

Ads for various products sold during the war. *Author's collection.*

cleaners." Watches were for sale at $30.00 at R.A. Burton Jewelry Co., Inc., and if a lady really wanted to look nice wearing her watch, she could go to Sallye Harmer Facial Studio and Beauty Salon to get a shampoo and wave for $0.75. There was even an ad that was musical:

> *If you want suds twice as speedy,*
> *Swan Soap is just what you needy,*
> *Compared with old-time floaters, Swan*
> *Is twice as fast and much more fun!*

The excitement of Christmas, however, could not erase from the minds of people that ships were being sunk in the North Atlantic, that German troops were occupying many European nations, that Japan had expanded its power in the east, that war preparations were taking place and that convoys were passing through the city on a regular basis. To put it another way, Richmonders prayed for peace but prepared for a war that seemed more and more inevitable. And then the inevitable happened.

Knowing nothing about what was going on half a world away, Richmonders awoke to a clear and moderately cold Sunday morning on December 7, 1941. Those who picked up the newspapers from their porches read this headline: "Roosevelt Sends Personal Message to Hirohito." It was seen as a last-ditch effort to stop a war with Japan. An editorial in the same paper commented, "The issue of peace or war with Japan hangs by a thread, and yet there may be no hostilities for weeks or months. The Japanese cannot back down openly before the United States, but they must know that they are virtually surrounded and extremely vulnerable if war comes." The writer concluded that "if a final showdown comes, war may yet be avoided, but if not, the United States must strike hard and quickly." Ironically, it was the Japanese, and not the United States, who were about to strike "hard and quickly."

As people prepared to eat breakfast and attend church or listen to the 11:00 a.m. services from St. Paul's Episcopal, Second Presbyterian or Grove Avenue Baptist on the radio, the Empire of Japan was launching its planes from aircraft carriers and setting course for the naval base at Pearl Harbor, Hawaii. Meanwhile, Richmonders read a comforting comment by James R. Young, a noted foreign correspondent, who wrote, "Actually the Japanese are no threat to any country of fighting consequence." While those reading the newspaper were finding comfort in this analysis, a Japanese pilot radioed, "Tora, Tora, Tora." And Japanese bombs and torpedoes smashed into the Pacific Fleet. Immediately, a message went out to the fleet: "Air Raid Pearl Harbor. This is no drill." While the fleet was being blasted and fires were raging, a chaplain on the USS *New Orleans* encouraged the struggling sailors, who were trying to lift the ammunition, with the cry, "Praise the Lord and pass the ammunition!"

Many Richmonders attended church and then returned home for the traditional large Sunday dinner. If they were listening to their radios, they had the choice of three programs that were being broadcast: *Quiet Harmonies* on WRNL, *World Today* on WRVA or *University of Chicago* on WMBG. At 2:26 p.m., radio listeners heard these heart-stopping words: "We interrupt this program to bring you a special news bulletin, 'The Japanese have attacked Pearl Harbor, Hawaii, by air, President Roosevelt has just announced.'" Yet not everyone was listening to a radio. They found out in other ways. My parents were window-shopping on Broad Street looking for Christmas gifts, and I was in my Taylor Tot (stroller) when a relative stopped his car and told them that the Japanese had attacked Pearl Harbor. Soon, a police officer stopped a sailor who was walking with his mother and told him that Pearl Harbor had been attacked. His mother burst into tears. Other people

The sinking of the USS *Arizona* during the Pearl Harbor attack. *National Archives.*

found out when movies were stopped and announcements were made in theaters. In one theater, three uniformed men were seen to quickly get up and leave. Those men already in the military service were ordered to their duty stations. While one sailor waited for a bus, he played "The Stars and Stripes Forever" on his harmonica. Nearby, a girl was crying as the 5:15 p.m. bus left the Greyhound Terminal for the Norfolk Naval Base. Before the day ended, Greyhound had run more than fifty special buses to get soldiers and sailors to their duty stations.

Infuriated by the sneak attack, local men immediately lined up at the Navy Recruiting Station to enlist. One man waiting to join the navy said, "I'm a pretty good shot and I want to take a shot at those Japs." Another young man seemed undecided, so the recruiter gave him an application and asked him if he wanted to fight. He filled out the application and returned it to the recruiter. He definitely wanted to fight.

Many of those already in the service left Richmond on trains departing from either Broad Street or Main Street Stations. For fear of missing their trains, servicemen pinned scraps of paper onto their uniforms with the time of their trains' departures. Volunteers would walk through the station, check the times, and wake the servicemen in time for them to catch their scheduled trains. Powerful locomotives pulled long lines of cars to the various military bases throughout the nation. As men boarded the trains, their families strained for final glances at loved ones. Then, the sounds of hissing steam, turning wheels, puffs of smoke and the ringing of a locomotive bell let everyone know that the train was leaving, and those left behind could only wave and pray for a safe return.

The *Richmond Times-Dispatch* published an extra edition on December 8. Newsboys yelled, "Extra, extra, read all about it! Japs attack Pearl Harbor!" When a reader opened the newspaper, he saw this headline: "Honolulu Bombed, Naval Battle Now Raging." In a random survey, most Richmonders believed the war had come with the Pearl Harbor attack, but some felt that the United States had forced the Japanese to attack because of its belligerent attitude and embargo. One optimistic person commented, "We can handle the Japanese in short order."

Later that Sunday, Richmonders watched the Twenty-ninth Infantry Division roll through the city. Bands played in Capitol Square and Monroe Park as the fourteen-thousand-man convoy drove through Richmond. A reporter commented, "The vehicles looked deadly efficient. Many had weapon carriers with a rifle tucked in a leather holster strapped near the drivers' hand. Others carried dummy anti-tank guns behind them, others carried gasoline." Most Richmonders would have preferred to see real weapons instead of fake ones. This was the only time in the war that a convoy made up of largely Virginians passed though Richmond. New mothers and other patients in the new Medical College of Virginia Hospital both heard and saw the convoy pass below them on Broad Street.

To protect vital highways, guards were immediately placed at the south end of the Lee Bridge and at other important installations like the water supply facilities, the Telephone Company building, public utilities and the gas works. While buildings were being guarded, labor unions called off their pickets, and airplane spotters began scanning the sky to see if enemy aircraft were coming toward Richmond. With war raging, no one knew if Richmond would be attacked; therefore, all kinds of precautions were being taken, but most of them would eventually prove unnecessary.

With the future of the American nation in peril and many of the ships anchored in Pearl Harbor still in flames, President Roosevelt spoke to a joint session of Congress on December 8, 1941. He opened with these words: "Yesterday, December 7, 1941—a date which will live in infamy—the United States of America was suddenly and deliberately attacked by the Naval and Air Forces of the Empire of Japan."

The president's speech was broadcasted on the radio in Richmond and was rebroadcasted over WRVA at 6:30 p.m. It was also broadcasted to students in the Richmond Public Schools. All classes were stopped at 12:30 p.m., and twenty-nine thousand pupils listened eagerly to the president's message. At Thomas Jefferson High School, there was a public address system, so all of the students heard the message in their classrooms. Following the attack and the speech, there were so many Bibles being sold that stores could not keep them in stock, and with good reason—the United States had declared war on Japan. Within days, Germany and Italy would declare war on the United States.

An editorial writer offered these comments:

> *America has been shocked into unity in a single Sunday afternoon. The bombs which came hurtling down without warning from Japanese warplanes upon our Pacific bases have closed the debate over the country's course. While the declaration of war will be directed against Tokyo, it will end all doubt that America is in this fight to the finish, not only against Japan, but also against her partners in crime, Germany and Italy. All three have left a trail of broken promises, crooked international dealings and savage persecutions without a parallel in modern times, and the dastardly attack by Japan on our Pacific bases must be answered tenfold.*

Correspondents sent their comments to be published in the newspapers. One writer proclaimed, "To Hell with those Japanese." Another writer suggested that "Hitler was like the snake in the Garden of Eden." One irate citizen took a slap at parties during the war. He wrote, "I am sure that many people here wonder if the debutantes will continue to spend so much time and money on coming out parties at this time, when thousands of our fine young men are fighting so desperately and giving their lives to defend our country." It was signed, "An American."

As Richmonders and the American nation prepared for war, more and more about the disaster at Pearl Harbor and other Pacific battlegrounds began filtering out. One story reported that an old battleship, believed to be the USS *Oklahoma*, had capsized, while a destroyer and many planes had been destroyed. This information was certainly not an accurate or complete report of the horrific disaster at Pearl Harbor, but it is doubtful if the American people could have absorbed the magnitude of the carnage at one time. After realizing that the Pearl Harbor attack was not a nightmare that would go away, Richmonders accelerated their preparations for war.

Following the attack, the America First Chapter was immediately disbanded. This organization, which was seeking to keep America out of the war, was meeting at the Jefferson Hotel when it received a telegram from its national office telling it to disband. A letter to the newspaper about the organization did not mince words. The writer fumed:

> *Our brilliant isolationist and noninterventionist groups and all their "fellow travelers" can thank themselves (no one else will) for the slaughtering and wounding of four hundred soldiers (who thought they were at peace) in the Hitler-instigated Japanese surprise attack on Pearl Harbor. No matter how madly they scramble onto the band-wagon and now shout for the war against the Japanese, we will never forget that* [Charles] *Lindberg and those who agreed with him are directly responsible for the murder of those service men.*

Lindbergh, it was reported, was in seclusion somewhere in New England.

Many letters were written to the local newspapers about the war. One writer noted, "In order to prosecute a successful war against our enemies, should not the leaders of our armed forces have a suitable background or ancestry?" There was a general feeling that those men who had ancestors who fought in the Confederate army would make excellent leaders in the current conflict. Several writers were concerned about the "flood of rumors originating in unknown sources and confusing or crippling the mental effectiveness of the nation." A mother commented, "In this time of stress, when, like thousands of other mothers, I find the strain of anxiety almost too much to bear, I am hoping that we can pass on to each other worthwhile thoughts that will take root in our minds and give us strength and courage as we go about our daily tasks." A final thought was that "Remember Pearl Harbor" should be our battle cry.

As a public service, the paper published the following information about air-raid signals: "Until the city gets a bigger siren then it has, air-raid warnings will be sounded by sirens of the Police and Fire Departments. The warning will be alternate long and short blasts sounded over a period of three minutes. The all clear, sounded on the same sirens, will consist of a series of short blasts over a period of five minutes."

On December 12, Richmonders learned that Germany and Italy had declared war on the United States. It was also reported that Air-Raid Warning Centers were going on a twenty-four-hour basis. The procedure for an air raid was as follows: "If an unidentified plane was spotted, it would be

The Nazi flag that flew over the conquered nations. *Canadian Archives.*

reported to the nearest Filter Center of the Aircraft Warning Service which will then transmit reports of unidentified planes to a center in Norfolk, Virginia, where the appropriate response would be determined."

Initially, Richmond had one observation post at Hotchkiss Field in the North Side and one at Three Chopt Road and Patterson Avenue in the West End. Other posts were planned for Drewery's Bluff, Brook Hill, Midlothian, Cold Harbor and Mechanicsville. Most of these centers were on porches of homes with immediate access to telephones. And if an enemy aircraft should reach Richmond, plans were revealed to protect inmates of the state penitentiary on Belvedere Street by putting them in the pipe tunnels around the institution. And on the University of Richmond campus, the Administration Building (Ryland Hall) was selected as an air-raid shelter. The building was perfect for this purpose since its ceiling was sixteen-inch-thick concrete, reinforced with steel and supported by steel girders. It was also noted that sandbags would be placed around the windows to protect against flying glass.

Whereas college students had a shelter, a man who lived in the city's West End wanted a private air-raid shelter constructed. He selected a shelter of the basement type "necessitating the strengthening of the basement walls." The Moline Machine Company, a British company, had a shelter ready for ninety persons at its Summit Avenue plant. The United States Post Office on Main Street had an air-raid shelter. One other bomb shelter was a little unusual.

W. Collier Gibson, a Jefferson Ward magistrate, had his own underground vault dug in Oakwood Cemetery. He watched the construction of the vault every day and already had his tombstone prepared.

In a nation searching for some good news, Richmonders, on December 12, learned that the Japanese battleship *Haurna* was sunk by three direct bomb hits by Captain Colin P. Kelly Jr. flying a B-17 Flying Fortress. Captain Kelly lost his life in the attack, but he managed to save his crew and became America's first war hero. The Richmond newspaper reminded its readers that Captain Kelly was the great-grandson of a Confederate captain who had died in battle. It was reported that "his young widow, whose eyes were shining with pride and not tears, kept repeating how proud she was of her husband and that their son would go to West Point like his father." (Subsequent information would reveal that the Japanese ship was not sunk, but at the time, Richmond needed good news whether fact or fiction.) One reporter wrote, "With such valor and fortitude to spur us on and the bravery of the men who battled through the blazing oil of Pearl Harbor to inspire it, America will win through to victory."

Less than a week after the Pearl Harbor attack and the declarations of war, there were instructions from the Office of Civilian Defense about what should be done in the event of an air raid. The steps were as follows:
Keep cool
Stay home
Put out lights
Lie down
Stay away from windows

On the first Sunday after the attack, people flocked to their houses of worship. There were a number of sermons that dealt with the war. At Memorial Methodist, J.G. Unruh spoke on the topic "What Can I Do," and at First Presbyterian, Walter Carson's sermon topic was "How Shall We Meet the Present Emergency?" The sermon topic by T. Rupert Coleman at Ginter Park Baptist was "War Has Come, So What?" and at St. John's Episcopal Church, where Patrick Henry proclaimed "Liberty or Death," E Company of the John Marshall High School Corps of Cadets attended the services along with the cadet band. Richmond's Jehovah's Witnesses met and reaffirmed that they would not salute the flag and declared that both "armies were instruments of the Devil." Many Jehovah's Witnesses suffered because of their beliefs.

As more and more men left their jobs and enlisted, women began to replace them in the workforce. One of their first jobs was learning to direct traffic as members of the Volunteer Motor Corps. In the 1940s, this was not a traditional job for women. Following instructions given at the Howitzer's Armory, the women began directing traffic in downtown Richmond as part of their training. One police officer reported that they encountered some difficulty teaching the ladies to blow their whistles loud enough to be heard over the noise of the traffic. During the next four years, men would get used to women doing many jobs formerly performed by males, including directing traffic.

On December 16, Richmonders learned more about the gravity of the loss at Pearl Harbor when it was reported that the battleship USS *Arizona* had been sunk and that many other ships had been damaged. The *Arizona* had been based at Norfolk, Virginia, on a number of occasions. But the government also reported that the Japanese attack had failed. No American aircraft carriers had been damaged, the Pacific Fleet was still a capable fighting force and vital repair facilities had not been destroyed. In retrospect, the attack unleashed a raging tiger that would eventually destroy the Japanese.

If the war news was bad, then the first air-raid alarm in Richmond was a disaster. A reporter wrote, "If you want to make a tactless remark of the first magnitude today, walk up to some staff member of the Richmond Office of Civilian Defense and say, 'It is a good thing that it was a false air-raid alarm yesterday because it showed that Richmond's general warning system isn't much good.'" One commentator said, "It was an alarm which failed to alarm." But Richmonders did learn that they needed some very loud sirens and that they should not rely on alarms on police cars and fire trucks.

There was also a report that the Richmond public schools would soon begin practicing air-raid drills during which students would leave their classes and go to a designated area of the school building. The principal of Springfield School in the East End advised other principals in a meeting that "preparations for possible air raids should not be taken lightly; and while most people don't expect bombers over Richmond, there is no guarantee that the city will escape attacks during the war. I remind you that Richmond is only twenty-five minutes by bomber from the coast."

Christmas began with the annual Christmas pageant, which took place at the State Capitol Building. The newspaper reported that "the Christmas angel's message of 'Peace on Earth and Good Will to Men' floated over Capitol Square last night, the first time in history that the city's annual Christmas pageant has opened on a world at war." Men and women in uniform stood next to civilians as they heard the ancient Christmas story. At the close of the program, a Christmas tree, decorated by Richmond firemen, was lit in Capitol Square.

Christmas 1941 was a beautiful day in Richmond. A Christmas editorial pointed out "the paradox of a world involved in war this Christmas at a time when all thoughts should be centered upon the Prince of Peace." Another writer offered the thought that "what we are fighting for is nothing less than the survival of the democratic impulse among the people of the world."

And Richmonders continued to prepare for war and to learn something of the sacrifices they would have to make. They learned that certain products would be difficult, if not impossible, to obtain. For example, all spare tires from new cars had to be removed and sent back to the factories from which they came. A spare tire was a luxury item since rubber was difficult to obtain. Soon, the tire recapping business became a big business. People were told that when tires wore out on delivery trucks, they would not be replaced. In many cases, home delivery of products would be a casualty of the war. And a bill was introduced in the General Assembly to make the stealing of an automobile tire a felony.

Women also had another problem. There was a silk stocking shortage. If the women learned that a certain store might have some silk stockings in stock, they would race to the store, attack the hosiery counter and sometimes get into fights over who might get the stockings that were available. But women did not need silk stockings to work in a gas station.

When a motorist pulled up to Nance's Service Station on Petersburg Pike to get gas, the driver was "amazed when a brown-haired woman in riding clothes removed the gas tank cap and stuck in the nozzle." The driver shouted, "Hey, I don't want any woman putting gas in my tank! A woman cannot do that right. Get a man." Mrs. Margaret Vaughan looked up and grinned, "I am the man around here." The driver looked perplexed for a moment. Then he laughed, "Well, I'll give anything a try once. Go ahead and do it."

There was major news at the end of the year in Richmond. The United States Patent Office was going to move from Washington, D.C., to Richmond. This was in conjunction with the government's plan to move some nonessential offices out of Washington to provide space for war-related departments. It was expected that 1,500 people would be employed in the office. Located in the Export Leaf Tobacco Company building (now a U-Haul facility) on Lombardy Street, this building was close to Broad Street and to Broad Street Station. The major concern regarding the move was that the building was recently painted a gleaming white, but as a wartime measure, buildings were supposed to be painted dark colors to make them less visible at night.

During the week after Christmas, mules were offered for sale to supplement automobiles. Available for sale at the South Richmond Stockyards were mules named Mouse Color Mare Mule, Buckskin Mare Mule and Mouse Horse Mule. The story concluded, "It is hoped that none of the mules will make an ass of himself and that Richmond's first mule sale will be something to bray about." It was also good to know that Richmond had maintained its leadership traditions by "pacing the nation in civil defense." Another positive note was that African Americans were joining in the war effort. This effort was led by the Negro Organizations Society.

As the year ended, the church bells of peace and the factory whistles of war merged to welcome 1942—a year that would see the nation walk through "the valley of the shadow of death."

CHAPTER 4

# KEEP CALM AND CARRY ON, 1942

*Praise the Lord and pass the ammunition*
*Praise the Lord and pass the ammunition*
*Praise the Lord and pass the ammunition*
*And we'll all stay free*
—*Frank Loesser*

January 1, 1942, was set aside by President Roosevelt as a day of prayer. In Richmond, an interdenominational service was held at St. Paul's Episcopal Church across from Capitol Square. St. Paul's had been the church of the Confederacy during the Civil War, and countless prayers had been offered by generations of Richmonders within its sacred walls. People folded their hands tightly on New Year's Day 1942, praying for the strength to endure a world war and for the safe return of their loved ones. Members of the city's faith communities were united in prayer as they walked from a place of peace into a world at war.

The impact of the war was quickly felt in Richmond. Colgate W. Darden, the newly elected governor, was sworn into office without any fanfare. It was his job to prepare Virginia for war. Although the war was thousands of miles away, no one knew if the Axis powers were capable of attacking Virginia. A Japanese submarine, *I-17*, had shelled some oil fields in California, and German U-boats were sinking ships off the coast of Virginia Beach. Could a U-boat sail up the James River and fire on Richmond, or did the Germans have airplanes that were capable of bombing East Coast cities, including Richmond? As Japan stormed across the Pacific, the newspapers did not help the situation by reminding Richmonders that they had sold steel to Japan, including the machinery from the old Pump House in Byrd Park.

The stress on the city was terrific. Everyone knew they had to do something, but what? People were confused, upset and unsure of their futures. And to add to the stress of life, more and more men were getting the following telegram: "Greetings: Having submitted yourself to a Local Board composed of your neighbors for the purpose of determining your availability for training and service in the armed forces of the United States, you are hereby notified that you have been selected for training and service in the Army." Once inducted into the service, their futures were under the control of the War Department.

How were families to live from day to day wondering if their homes might be bombed or if loved ones would ever come home—alive? Although Richmonders were unsure about what to do, they were determined to do their part to avenge the attack on Pearl Harbor, as well as to save Europe from Hitler's goose-stepping legions. An editorial writer commented, "America has her back to the wall."

One thing that Richmonders and the rest of the nation could do was to organize victory rallies to build morale and support for the war. In early 1942, there was a rally at the Mosque, where Governor Darden reminded those in the audience that the United States faced its "most dangerous military alliance in history." Rallies could lift sprits and men could be drafted, but more needed to be done. One of the first steps was to plan and implement blackouts to protect the city from aerial attacks like the ones taking place almost daily in Europe. Accordingly, the first blackout of 1942 was planned for February 9.

The purpose of a blackout was to make sure a city could not be seen at night if bombers should arrive. It was reported that

> *sometime between the hours of 8 and 10 p.m. on the selected date* [February 9] *sirens will wail in Richmond, and air-raid wardens, fire watchers, auxiliary fireman and policemen will rush to their designated posts and all other units in the defense setup will turn out for possible action. The blackout will remain in effect for not more than thirty minutes and may end in fifteen minutes.*

Since air-raid sirens were still not available, the city once again relied on the sirens on police and fire vehicles. In all jurisdictions, air-raid wardens had the responsibility of seeing that all persons got off the streets and that no lights were showing. All traffic, except emergency vehicles, must stop.

Richmonders were given the following instructions:

*If you are in your home when you hear the alert, your only duty is to see that no lights are showing from the outside. Put out lights everywhere except in the blackout room. Windows must be covered so there is no light showing. To prevent light from showing, dark shades, heavy curtains, oilcloth, blankets, heavy paper and black paint should be used. Flashlights can be used as long as they are not pointed at a window.*

It was suggested that dogs and cats should be put in a room separate from members of the family during an air raid because they might get upset at all of the noise and bite family members. One animal that was not covered in the instructions was the possum seen running on North Twentieth Street in Richmond's Church Hill. It was suggested by someone that he could always "play possum" in an air raid.

As the time got closer for the blackout, it was announced that all Richmond radio stations would notify their listeners of the blackout along with the sirens. Richmonders were also advised that station WRNL would broadcast a description of the blackout from the top of the Central National Bank Building on Broad Street. The mayor reminded the people that the test was not expected to be perfect but would be used to "educate and prepare the public for a future all-out blackout." He also advised everyone to be careful and to remember that "this is no show. It is a serious matter and should be considered as such."

On February 9 at 9:01 p.m., Richmond had its much-anticipated first wartime blackout, and it was initially judged by officials as being excellent and 90 percent effective. A military observer stood on top of the Central National Bank Building to critique the effectiveness of the blackout. The analysis was that "to get a city the size of Richmond to accomplish what it has accomplished is really remarkable." But later, the army, in a follow-up report, stated, "If a plane from Langley Field had been an enemy bomber its crew would have had little difficulty in picking their target." Richmonders knew they still had work to do.

An irate woman wrote a letter to the editor of the newspaper and really let people know what she thought about the blackout. She complained that

she never heard the alarm from the fire engines and police cars, and she further stated that a radio announcement would do her no good. She wrote, "This recalcitrant individual is one of those who are strongly inclined to regard the radio, except on special occasions, as one of the pleasant and attractive devices of the devil to stupefy the mass mind and discourage as far as possible all original thinking."

It was not a time to joke about air raids and the war, but someone passed around a mimeographed memorandum with the title "What to do in an Aerial Raid." The paper provided the following suggestions:

*If you find an unexploded bomb, always pick it up and shake it like hell. Maybe the firing pin is stuck. If that doesn't work, heave it into the furnace. The Fire Department will come later and take care of things.*

*If an incendiary bomb is found burning in a building, throw gasoline on it. You can't put it out anyway, so have a little fun.*

*Take advantage of opportunities afforded you when air-raid sirens sound. If you are in a tavern grab some beer, or if you are in a taxi or watching a movie, grab a blonde.*

The FBI was not amused by this, but there is no record of the malefactor being apprehended.

In addition to blackouts, airplane observation posts were staffed around the clock. Early in the year, the post at Patterson Avenue and Three Chopt Road was shifted to the roof of the Chemistry Building (Puryear Hall) at the University of Richmond. The visibility from the roof was deemed to be very good in all directions. University of Richmond faculty, staff and students staffed the post for two-hour shifts during the broiling sun or pouring rain. As more and more college men entered the service, Westhampton College women began to staff the post. It was reported that this was an excellent opportunity for "women to show that they are interested in the defense of their country." In fact, efforts were made at Westhampton College to "kill off the last survivors of the catch-me-quick-I-think-I-am-going-to-faint type of girl who flourished in the days of the hoop skirt and bustle." Miss Fanny

*Opposite, top*: The Central National Bank Building, which was used by the mayor and military officials as a lookout to determine the success of blackouts. *Photograph by Walter Griggs.*

*Opposite, bottom*: Puryear Hall, where University of Richmond students, staff and faculty stood watch for enemy airplanes. *Photograph by Walter Griggs.*

G. Crenshaw, director of physical education at the college, affirmed, "Not only is it no longer fashionable, but it's not even patriotic, in these days to be helplessly feminized." She continued, "Women have their part to do in the winning of the war and they can't work strenuously for long hours at difficult tasks unless they are physically fit." Soon, women were seen climbing hand-over-hand up ropes attached to the gymnasium ceiling. It was noted that these women would now have the strength to throw a bomb off the roof of a college building. A concluding remark was that faculty members would reprimand "spine-sitting" and poor posture in class. The motto was: "Stand up Straight for Uncle Sam." In addition to seeking to strengthen the student body, there were also efforts to provide mental strengthening for the war effort. The University of Richmond and the Richmond Professional Institute of the College of William and Mary both began to offer courses to aid in the war effort.

War brought about censorship of the news, as well as censorship of the weather forecast, which began in late 1941. Generally, newspapers were limited to reporting the weather within a 150-mile radius of a city. A typical weather forecast was printed on the first page of the paper. One forecast was as follows: "Scattered showers and thunderstorms, somewhat cooler in the interior." Radio weather forecasts were censored to prevent enemy submarines from learning of current weather conditions in the United States. Although these restrictions were designed to protect the nation, Groundhog's Day provided the opportunity for a little humor.

The following conversation was reported when Mr. Groundhog squeaked, "I'm not talking. I might give aid and comfort to the enemy." Mr. Groundhog continued, "In my position, I cannot afford to talk. I bet those Japs would give a mess of money to know what I did. Well, here's how I'm working it, see? I'm having a barbed-wire fence put around my hole and a small American flag on top of it." When last seen, Mr. Groundhog had ducked back into his hole.

Americans could not jump into a hole, but they did change the way to keep time. On February 9, 1942, President Roosevelt put the United States on year-round daylight saving time or, as it was called, "War Time." Virginia was in the Eastern War Time Zone. In order to help Richmonders adjust to the new time, there were several articles in the newspaper to explain the transition. Instructions were as follows: "Remember to turn clocks and watches ahead one hour before retiring for the evening." In some areas of Virginia, schools would now start at 10:00 a.m. instead of 9:00 a.m. "in order that farm children may complete their chores before boarding school buses."

In addition to getting used to getting up an hour earlier, Richmond merchants were actively supporting the war effort by selling War Bonds and War Saving Stamps. War Bonds were issued by the federal government to help finance the war and could be purchased for less than nineteen dollars. For those individuals who could not afford to purchase a bond, War Savings Stamps were available for as little as ten cents. These stamps were largely marketed to schoolchildren, who put them in little stamp books. During the war, there would be frequent bond rallies to sell bonds. Posters appeared with these slogans: "Buy Bonds Today," "Your Bonds Buy Ships," "Back the Attack, Buy War Bonds" and "Convert Your Cash to Bombs and Shells, Buy War Bonds."

Thalhimers and Miller and Rhoads were the two major department stores on Broad Street in the 1940s. Early in 1942, a window of Thalhimers had an American flag in it, along with patriotic posters. One poster warned, "Careless Talk Loses Lives." At the same time, Miller and Rhoads converted its premier window, a corner window at Sixth and Grace Streets, into a Victory Window. It was decorated in red, white and blue and became "a glass sales booth with a door and steps that opened onto the street." The store's management reported that the "window will no longer be used for display merchandise but to sell War Bonds and Stamps." Governor Colgate Darden arrived at "the Victory Window" and bought the first stamp. To further promote bond sales, the store ran the following ad: "We do need to emphasize that War Stamps and Bonds are the best things we have to sell, that is why the most important window in our store has been turned into an office for the duration."

There was a major news story in February when it was reported that a shipyard would be built in Richmond. The navy purchased the site formerly occupied by the Richmond Car Works at the end of Fourth Street in South Richmond and planned to lease a site close to the Richmond Deepwater Terminal for the shipyard. Then, on April 30, it was announced by Senator Harry F. Byrd of Virginia that the shipyard was cancelled. Richmonders took the demise of the shipyard in stride but regretted all of the federal government funds that were used for no purpose. Although Richmond did not get the shipyard, it did get the headquarters of the Anti-Aircraft Command, which was established at the Mosque in April. With but a few exceptions, the headquarters would command all antiaircraft artillery and barrage balloon units in the United States. Richmonders could easily see the large moving vans of Barrett's Transfer and Storage parked outside the Mosque being unloaded.

Then the grim reality of war stared newspaper readers in the face when pictures of the first two Richmonders to die in combat were printed in the paper. The two servicemen were Lieutenant George Ben Johnston Handy of the United States Army and Fireman Third Class Julian Callaway Booth of the United States Coast Guard. Ben Handy was killed in the Philippines while serving with General MacArthur, and Julian Callaway died in action at sea. These deaths, along with the sinking of ships off the Virginia coast, brought the war very close to home, especially when the survivors of the sunken ships were brought to Norfolk.

During the war, Richmonders put flags in their windows with blue stars on them, one for each member of the family who was serving their country. In some homes, there were several blue stars on display. If someone who lived in the house was killed, the blue star was replaced by a gold star. Many blue stars turned to gold during the war. Just by walking down the street, you knew the homes where a family member was fighting for, or had died for, his country.

While Richmonders were dying in combat, the city was still having difficulty with its air-raid sirens. Hardly a day passed without a story about the sirens—or lack thereof. Anxious citizens were finally advised that the new sirens were beginning to arrive. On April 4, the newspaper reported that "Richmond's eleven new air-raid sirens unlimbered their iron lungs for the first time at noon today to blast open the United States Defense Bonds and Stamps Pledge Campaign, but the blast failed to materialize in the downtown sections where nary a whisper was heard." Why? A reporter suggested, "There must have been an insect colony in the 'daddy' of Richmond's sirens at Ninth and Broad Streets. It did not emit a note of the warbling warning sound." The good news was that the other sirens placed throughout the city seemed to function perfectly.

The city government continued to test the sirens almost daily, and by the end of April, Richmond had seventeen sirens in place, and eight more were still on order. Even though most sirens were working, one siren did not work for an unusual reason. A reporter wrote, "Northside Richmonders were 'getting the bird' instead of an air-raid warning." The air-raid siren at Laburnum Avenue and Brook Road did not function. Why? Workman found that "birds had moved in and were busily engaged in building a nest inside." To avoid this sort of problem in the future, screens were placed over all sirens. But the bird problem was nothing compared to the uproar raised by a New Yorker, who commented that southern accents were detrimental to vocal air-raid warnings. Although the Civil War had ended in 1865, Richmonders were still sensitive about negative comments from a "Yankee."

Ration books and related material. *Judith Reynolds Johnson Collection.*

Local residents had seen the successes and failures of blackouts and the problems with the sirens. Now, they faced another challenge: the implementation of rationing that was designed to make sure available products were made available on both the homefront and on the battlefield. Each person was issued a ration book filled with stamps for various rationed items. To purchase a rationed item, you needed both money and the appropriate ration stamps or tokens. In the years ahead, rationing would cover more and more products, get more complicated, cause a measure of irritation and give rise to a black market in rationed goods.

Because of the shortage of rubber, tires were the first item rationed. Frustrated Richmonders saw their tires wear out, but replacements were not available. To get new tires required filing out a questionnaire with fourteen divisions, with some divisions having as many as fourteen questions. However, Richmonders were warned that after answering all of these questions and having an inspection of the current tires, the chances of getting new tires approached zero.

Since they were difficult to obtain, thieves started stealing tires off cars and selling them on the black market or using them themselves. In one case,

An advertisement promoting the payment of legal prices. *Carolyn Whitworth Brittain Collection.*

thieves went into a garage behind a man's house on Fourth Avenue and stole his tires. In another case, tires were stolen off a car parked in a parking lot in the 700 block of East Marshall Street. And to make matters worse, there was a ban on recapping tires unless the inner tube from the old tire was serviceable. And if everything was in order, it still might take a couple weeks to get a tire recapped.

Gas rationing hit every Richmonder with a car when it was implemented in May 1942. Cars were issued stickers depending on the needs of the driver. An "A" sticker was issued to drivers whose cars were deemed nonessential. The "B" sticker went to drivers considered essential to the war effort, such as industrial workers. If you were a physician, minister or railroad worker, you

*Left*: Carolyn Whitworth saving gas by riding a pony. *Carolyn Whitworth Brittain Collection.*

*Below*: A goat pulling a cart to save gasoline. *Photograph by Dorothy Griggs.*

were assigned a "C" sticker. "X" stickers went to members of Congress and people deemed important. The amount of gas allocated would vary from time to time during the course of the war. And since gas was scarce, it was not long before the Richmond police reported the first theft of gasoline, as well as counterfeit stickers. The first theft occurred when thieves drained ten gallons of gas from a car parked in front of an apartment in the 100 block of North Stafford Avenue.

To deal with the shortage of gasoline, Miller and Rhoads Department Store, after a quarter of a century of using trucks, began using "Victory Wagons," better known as horses and wagons. It was suggested that the "clip-clop of the horses' hoofs and the rumble of the wagons would be patriotic noises for the vehicles would run on iron tires and their motive power would be fed by oats and hay, not gasoline." The first wagon was used for deliveries in the central city, and when more wagons arrived, they would be used throughout the city.

Although tires and gas were in short supply, church attendance increased during 1942. The *Virginia Methodist Advocate* suggested that "people were going to church since they did not have enough gas to get away on the weekends." If a person wanted to ride a bike to church, new regulations stated that they could no longer acquire full-sized bikes. No bike with a frame over seventeen inches could be sold. If a person did not want to attend church, it was reported that golf courses were seeing more players and that movies were a popular diversion even though many of them were war movies.

There was also an emphasis on visits to local places of interest to save both gas and tires. One suggestion was to visit Hollywood Cemetery. If a person did not want to look at graves, he or she could watch the trains go down the tracks next to the James River. Other suggestions included eating watermelon in Bryan Park, feeding ducks in Byrd Park, letting children drink from a water fountain dedicated to the temperance movement, visiting St. John's Church or squirrel watching. A reporter wrote that he watched "two squirrels send children into gales of laughter as the squirrels chased each other through the back and front door of their little green house in a nearby tree." Mention was also made of monuments and historic buildings as being places to visit. There was a campaign to "See Virginia First."

When families returned home from duck feeding and squirrel watching, they returned to homes where almost everything was rationed. Since the government wanted all available aluminum for national defense, new refrigerators could have only one ice tray. Milk companies started making milk deliveries every other day; canned pineapple could no longer be found; alarm clocks were difficult to obtain because everyone needed them to get up on time; to obtain a new tube of toothpaste you had to turn in an empty tube; razor blades were restricted to one per week; and workers in state offices were told to use both sides of the stationery in writing letters and to use pencils until the stubs wore out.

As more women replaced men in the workforce, there was an extensive review of the changes in the Richmond employment picture since Pearl Harbor was attacked. It was pointed out that in March 1941, there were about six ads per day for women for the following jobs: bookkeepers, cashiers, stenographers and waitresses. A year later, there were over fifty ads per day for women. Positions now included a long list of jobs that had formally been the domain of men. Examples included the following: diaper delivery drivers, bakery salesladies, taxi drivers and women to help on aviation tours. Soda jerks who could give a "feminine flip" to ice cream were also in demand. A supervisor at DuPont hired many women, and of their work he commented, "They're okeh [sic]." A final observation in the newspaper was that "it is a far cry from the days of pinafores and parasols."

Some male supervisors claimed that female workers tended to be unstable. Stable or unstable, there was a campaign to encourage women to work in war-related jobs. Some of the slogans were as follows: "Do the Job He Left Behind," "The More Women Work, the Sooner We Will Win," "We Can Do It," "Join Us in a Victory Job" and "Women There's Work to Be Done and a War to Be Won." Women who were in the workforce were personified by a character known as "Rosy the Riveter."

Many companies had a romance problem. One supervisor commented, "You find that everywhere. Sometimes it's just a matter of a young and inexperienced foreman and rather aggressive girls." It was also suggested that "an occasional girl just uses the talents she was born with to make headway. We don't mind as long as it doesn't interfere with production." One man commented that he had hired two girls, but both quit. One quit to marry a soldier, and one quit to go back home. To complete the story, the man who hired them got drafted.

In state government, the influx of women raised a new issue: could they wear socks to work since nylons were rationed and almost impossible to obtain? It was decided by the governor of Virginia that socks were acceptable, but everyone seemed to be waiting for the first woman with the courage to wear them to work in the State Capitol Building. Apparently, the name of the first "socked" woman has been lost to history; therefore, her monument is not in Capitol Square.

Men who were working in office buildings were getting used to a change in style. Beginning in 1942, cuffs on men's suits were eliminated. It was also reported that in the near future, vests with double-breasted suits and long suit coats would be eliminated, along with patch pockets, pleats and two-trouser suits. One merchant observed that "men are slower to react to changes in clothes than women, but they were concerned about the elimination of cuffs on pants." A few creative men sought to circumvent the new regulations by ordering suits without alternations and then adding cuffs or buying the material and paying someone to make the suits.

Clothing was only a minor problem compared to another problem facing both men and women. Some women were being arrested on morals charges. Based on a complaint from Camp Lee in Petersburg that "many soldiers on leave were being infected with social diseases in Richmond," police staged a series of raids on four hotels. The hotels raided were the following: the Travelers' Hotel, the William Byrd Hotel, the Virginia Hotel and the Gilbert Hotel. A number of men were arrested for soliciting for prostitution, and several prostitutes were also arrested. Even after the raid, Camp Lee authorities "were still vocal and loud in their condemnation of 'contact places' in Richmond because of an ever-increasing number of social infections reported to them by the camp medical authorities." To quiet the authorities at Camp Lee and to enhance morality in Richmond, the police chief said there were ongoing efforts to trap the solicitors who were frequently acting as bellhops. If the advice of one Richmond pastor had been followed, there would have been fewer problems with reckless behavior. The Reverend O.A. Sauer once said, "Don't go any place you do not want to be found dead." I suspect no one would want to be found dead in a house of prostitution.

Although there was a concern about "love birds" getting out of control, Richmond's pigeons were ready to serve their nation. Two hundred of Richmond's finest homing pigeons joined the Army Signal Corps and were deployed in combat zones. Even though there were modern methods of communication, "pigeons still played an important role in military maneuvers, because they could get through when other means of communication failed." One writer summarized the pigeon enlistments with the comment: "Coo-Coo, You-All-Pigeons from Virginia, join the Army." It is a beautiful thought that the bluebirds flying over the "White Cliffs of Dover" in England were now joined by Richmond's pigeons.

This pigeon might be a relative of Homer of World War II fame. *Photograph by Walter Griggs.*

Pigeons also took part in various bond and scrap drives by representing doves of peace. On one occasion, "pigeons fluttered upward while a male choir sang the 'Recessional.'" One very special pigeon was assigned to carry a special message to President Roosevelt. Pigeons did not use gasoline, so it was an inexpensive way to send a message to the president—and surely, pigeons could refuel at a birdfeeder en route to the White House.

Homer was one pigeon that stayed in Richmond. The story began when a navy recruiter, who was working in the Parcel Post Building on Main Street, noticed a pigeon walking on the window ledge. The pigeon pecked the glass, and the yeoman on duty opened the window. The pigeon strutted in dressed in gray and blue plumage that could almost pass for navy blue. After getting acquainted, the navy recruiter on duty would call, "Ho-o-o-omer, soups on." If he was in the area, Homer would flutter in and sit on the nearest desk. At last report, Homer was being considered for advanced flight training.

One war effort that became popular all over Richmond was the Victory Garden. Virtually every piece of vacant land was turned into a mini farm. To keep enthusiasm from getting out of control, it was urged that shrubbery and lawns not be dug up. There were even Victory Gardens at the Union Theological Seminary and the University of Richmond. Food not used by a

Walter Griggs and his dog, Cookie, in their backyard with the grapevines that were planted for the war effort. *Photograph by Dorothy Griggs.*

family or an institution was used for school lunch programs. The Reverend Arthur W. Newell of St. John's Evangelical Lutheran Church used the Victory Garden to convey a spiritual message to his congregation. He wrote, "God has chosen an emergency to draw us closer to Him. We can be drawn back to a deeper faith in Him and to a better understanding of the men of the soil who till for us daily. Thank God for a [Victory] Garden and for His loving care for us and all men and women, always."

While Richmonders were preparing the homefront for war, the news from the combat zones was dismal. The United States was being pushed off the islands in the Pacific, and the war in Europe was still raging. Then Richmonders awoke to some good news. Finally, the *Richmond News Leader* of April 18, 1942, reported, "The Japanese command announced that hostile war planes bombed Tokyo, Yokohama, Nagoya, and Kobe today and caused air-raid alarms to sound on the four main islands of Japan." Japanese observers said that the raiders over Tokyo bore the insignia of the United States. This was the first air raid that Japan had experienced. It was later disclosed that Lieutenant Colonel James H. Doolittle was the leader of the raid. Although most Richmonders were pleased with the attack, some people felt Japan might try to bomb the United States as an act of reprisal. Regardless of the consequences to America, there would be many more attacks on Japan and the other Axis nations in the years ahead.

A lot of people wondered where the bombers had come from, but President Roosevelt only responded, "Shangri-La." (In 1944, the United States would commission an aircraft carrier named the USS *Shangri-La*, and it would be christened by Mrs. James H. Doolittle.) In retrospect, the raid did little physical damage to Japan, but it was a great boost to morale in the United States and made the Japanese people feel less secure. In a sense, it was a partial retribution for the attack on Pearl Harbor, where battleships were still in the mud, leaking oil and serving as the final resting place of hundreds of sailors. With this raid, Pearl Harbor was remembered.

Weather forecasts were censored because of wartime regulations; therefore, people did not know what to wear for the traditional Easter Parade. Still, most Richmonders went to church, partook of a meal and then paraded down the street. What made this parade different was the large number of men and some women in uniform who joined the parade. It was pointed out, however, that "many civilian women had gay-flowered feminine hats and [wore] corsages on their shoulders." There were no reports of seeing the Easter Bunny dressed as a sailor.

Around this same time, there was an article in the *Richmond News Leader* about the surrender of Robert E. Lee at Appomattox Court House. In the article, a connection was made between the present conflict and the Civil War. It was observed that "it was a strange coincidence that on the seventy-seventh anniversary of Lee's surrender at Appomattox, the War Department should issue the sad communiqué that a message has been received from General Jonathan Wainwright advising that the defenses of Bataan had been overcome." During the Battle of Bataan, a soldier commented that "there are no atheists in foxholes." And General Douglas MacArthur promised, "I shall return." When Corregidor fell to the Japanese, the *Richmond Times-Dispatch* suggested that "every American should stand today with bared head, remembering the heroism of the men and women who fought so desperately in the Philippines." To continue the fight, there was another bond drive and a visit from Dorothy Lamour, a well-known movie star.

On May 13, the Hotel John Marshall was jam-packed to await Lamour's arrival from Main Street Station. When she made her appearance, someone screamed, "Boys, she is here!" A reporter commented that "Miss Lamour looks luscious on the screen, but there's nothing like the third dimension to give that young woman more oomph than should be paraded before the naked eye." James Jackson Kilpatrick wrote, "A delegation of marines, soldiers, and sailors stuck to Dottie like butter to a plate and Miss Lamour sold $1,100,000 worth of bonds." Kilpatrick continued, "She wore a black outfit which fitted as if someone had melted her up and poured her in, and she looked twice as luscious as she looks on screen." Miss Lamour's visit was a real morale builder.

And then there was good news from the war. The *Richmond News Leader*'s headlines proclaimed, "Jap Invasion Fleet Smashed in the Battle of the Coral Sea." Although little information was provided, Richmonders knew the United States had stopped the Japanese attempt in early May to invade Port Moresby, located in New Guinea. This was the first check on the Japanese advance since Pearl Harbor. And it was a battle between aircraft carriers; the two fleets never saw each other. In this battle, Ensign John Wingfield, a Richmonder and a graduate of both John Marshall High School and the University of Virginia, was killed in an effort to sink a Japanese ship. His mother received the Navy Cross awarded him, and eventually a navy destroyer escort would be named in his honor. It was in this same battle that the Japanese aircraft carrier *Shoho* was hit, and Lieutenant Commander Robert E. Dunn radioed to the USS *Lexington* the still remembered phrase, "Scratch One Flattop."

This battle was followed in early June by the Battle of Midway, which cost the Japanese four irreplaceable aircraft carriers. There were many heroes in this battle, which turned the tide in the Pacific in favor of the Americans. The United States lost the aircraft carrier USS *Yorktown*, but this was not disclosed to the American public immediately. Richmonders were excited and grateful for the victory over the Japanese navy, the same navy that had attacked Pearl Harbor on the "Day of Infamy."

John Everett Lindsay Jr., of radio station WRNL, was not in combat. He was in Richmond making pro-Nazi comments at the corner of Meadow and Main Streets. When arrested, he said he was just kidding. The reporter spent a night in jail on the charge of "carrying on un-American activities and being an enemy sympathizer." After reflecting on his stunt while in jail, he was released the next morning. The next caper occurred when two newspaper reporters posed as Nazis in front of Lee's monument. They suffered the same fate, although they claimed it was only a joke. Police officers did not have much of a sense of humor with the nation in peril.

Then, things got serious. It was reported that a class of four hundred naval trainees would begin studying at the Navy Diesel School in Richmond. Before the end of the war, enrollment would rise to two thousand. It was hoped that much of the material purchased for the failed shipyard could be used in the Diesel School. However, the sailors had too much time on their hands, and it was not long before a restaurant on West Broad Street and another on Hull Street were declared "out of bounds" to the sailors at the school. The media did not report the names of the establishments, but apparently fights broke out in both of them.

Cigars became very hard to find because of rationing. It was suggested that cigar smokers of the world should unite and "Slap the Jap." (I can still remember that my grandfather was an avid cigar smoker. Instead of throwing the butt of the cigar away, he would put cigar butts on the hot water pipes in the basement and let the heat dry them out. Then he would smoke the cigar butts. I have often wondered if some of those cigar butts from the 1940s might still be drying out in that basement.)

It takes a real man to smoke a cigar, and it takes a really strong woman to get married while a war is being fought. Dorothy Janet Dowd was not such a woman. She and Private Claude Leonard Moore went to city hall to get a marriage license. While waiting, she fainted three times. She was caught by city magistrate J.H. Binford Peay and others before she hit the floor. Her husband-to-be said that this was the second marriage for both of them. They had been divorced for about three months before deciding to marry each other again. Wars do strange things to people.

July 4, 1942, was celebrated at the City Stadium. Combat teams with weapons arrived, and throughout the afternoon, guns were fired to save the cost of pop crackers and fireworks. A reporter wrote as follows, "In City Stadium 155 millimeter antitank guns, hand grenades, and bombs were making the Old Dominion sound like Dunkirk." He also commented that "fetching young things appeared on Main Street to sell Defense Stamps and did a roaring business following the celebration."

While cannons were rocking Richmond on July 4, the Richmond Army Air Base was being completed. It had three thousand men, but no planes were on the site, which was adjacent to, and included, the Richard Evelyn Byrd Flying Field. Sentries were in place and had fired on a car that tried to get onto the base. It was an honest error on the part of the driver, and he was not hurt. To make the servicemen feel at home on the base, the "top sergeants made the soldiers build little ornamental fences, walks and signs with such names as 'Hitler's Misery Camp,' 'Flying Grease Monkeys,' 'Horizontal Inn' and so on." The initial mission of the base was special flight training.

To protect the Richmond Air Base from attack, a decoy airfield was built in proximity to fool any Nazis who planned to bomb the real air base. A lot of mystery still surrounds this project, and some remains of it can still be found if you know where to look.

And there were more scrap drives. Richmonders were told that fat and oils should be saved because they contained glycerin, which was essential

*Left*: A wartime poster urging people to save scrap. *National Archives*.

*Below*: German Howitzer like the one donated by the City of Richmond to the War Department. *Author's collection*.

to the manufacture of a wide variety of explosives. Housewives were asked to save all of their waste fats and grease from pan drippings and then take them to the meat dealers who would pay for them. If grease was taken to the store and other purchases made, consumers were admonished not to use a second-hand bag. The city health inspectors termed this "one of the most unsanitary practices imaginable." There were many slogans associated with saving fat, including "Save Waste Fat for Explosives" and "We Want Your Kitchen Waste."

In another salvage drive, there was an interesting story of how the Seaboard Railway was going to support the war effort. It was reported that "thousands of tons of steel rail used for reinforcing railroad crossings between Richmond and Florida would be ripped up by the railroad and turned over to the War Production Board." A railroad spokesman pointed out that there were ninety-eight rails buried in the Hermitage Road crossing alone. The City of Richmond contributed to the salvage drive by donating an old steam engine that had been in the basement of city hall. But the ultimate donation came courtesy of the Kaiser's Army from World War I.

A captured German howitzer had been on display at the intersection of Idlewood Avenue and Shepphard Street near Byrd Park since 1926. A reporter wrote, "A German gun which, during the last war, roared out its song of hate against the Allies will very shortly render an encore—this time on the Allies' side." The eight-ton German howitzer was given by the City of Richmond to army ordnance officials to be scrapped and made into parts for a General Lee M3 medium tank. The war trophy was loaded on a truck, carried up the Boulevard, circled around the "Stonewall" Jackson monument and carried down Broad Street to the Frank H. Knott junkyard. The truck carrying the howitzer had metal license plates, but by 1943, all license plates would be made of fiber to save metal.

While a howitzer was being scrapped from World War I, a plywood model of the CSS *Merrimac*, the famous Confederate ironclad from the Civil War, was opened at Sixth and Broad Streets to serve as a naval recruiting center. The model was twelve by forty feet and would soon become a Richmond landmark.

Moving howitzers and building ships on Broad Street raised little controversy, but an issue regarding women's dress was quite controversial. The issue: must girls wear hose to dances? On one side of the issue were two hundred girls who wanted to attend dances without stockings. Some chaperones thought it might be acceptable to attend without hose "if their legs are well tanned or they used a tanning lotion." Other chaperones argued that "hose make the girls look so much prettier and neater and even a good leg makeup is apt to smear." Another chaperone had heard "comments from soldiers about girls who attend dances without hose." The debate continued until hose were no longer available. One British sailor, who was visiting Richmond, made several comments about Richmond women. He said that "American girls have it all over their British sisters in glamour and all that sort of thing." He did not mention hose, but he endeared himself by not complaining about American tea.

Young women working in the Selective Service headquarters in the State Office Building did not have the problem of the dancers. They had already given up hose for the duration and had begun to wear mercerized cotton mesh stockings. It was reported that "young men are inspecting the—er, ah—legs of the Selective Service girls, and are finding them still attractive, although clothed in cotton."

Then the news turned to the invasion of the Solomon Islands by the United States Marines under the command of Major General Alexander A. Vandergrift, a native Virginian from Charlottesville. The *Richmond Times-Dispatch* reported, "Good news comes from the first large-scale American offensive in the Pacific. But it is now being brought home to us how costly these offensives will be and what rivers of blood must be poured out as we regain the vital areas we have lost." So many ships were lost during the battle that an area was called "Iron Bottom Sound." United States Navy ships still drop a wreath in the area on the anniversary of the battle. This invasion was part of the American strategy to move from island to island until they reached Japan.

Next, the United States Army Air Force Flying Fortresses made their first European air raid. Richmonders were proud to learn that Colonel Frank A. Armstrong of Richmond had been one of the leaders in this initial all-American attack on Fortress Europe. These attacks, with Americans bombing during the day and the British at night, caused Edward R. Murrow to term these bombing missions an "Orchestrated Hell." For the rest of the war, men would fly their "Flying Fortresses," "Liberators" and "Lancaster" bombers on bombing raids over enemy territory in an effort to blast Hitler's Germany back to the Stone Age. At the same time, the German 88s and other weapons made the Allies pay dearly for their efforts. It is a horrible thing to see a plane filled with one's fellow airmen explode in midair with no sign of any parachutes.

To support the homefront while the men were fighting, Joe Ukrop closed his Hull Street grocery store at noon once a week. The *Richmond News Leader* reported, "Six clerks piled into the grocer's truck and went to the farm of Mr.

A U.S. Army Air Force patch designed by Walt Disney. *Author's collection.*

Ukrop's father, where they cut and harvested two and a half acres of corn."
It was all part of a plan that the Hull Street grocer had announced when he
said that his store would be closed each Wednesday afternoon for six weeks
while he and his employees helped Chesterfield and Henrico County farmers
harvest their crops. Mrs. Ukrop said that she avoided sunburn by wearing the
largest straw hat you've ever seen. The newspapers would frequently report on
this effort and even let the readers know if the store had to close on another
day because it rained on Wednesday. Before long, Mr. Ukrop's customers
joined the effort. Other efforts to help farmers came from Chandler Junior
High School, where its students became "farmers for a day" by going to farms
in Varina to harvest corn that would otherwise be lost.

Since 1915, John Marshall High School had had a corps of cadets
that was not only a source of community pride but had also rendered
valuable service during World War II. As a war measure, a cadet corps

Monument in honor of the John Marshall Corps of Cadets. *Photograph by Cara F. Griggs.*

was established at rival Thomas Jefferson High School in September 1942 with over five hundred cadets. Although equipment and uniforms were difficult to obtain and the cadets used wooden rifles, the corps drilled every morning and became more and more proficient. The cadets learned to march, carry rifles and memorize their guard orders. (Many years later, I was in the Thomas Jefferson Corps of Cadets, and I can still remember marching down Oakwood Avenue with World War II rifles while the cadet band played the "Colonel Bogey March.")

It was also in September that the issue of the Capitol Square fence surfaced. The fence was originally installed to keep pigs, cows and other assorted livestock out of Capitol Square. Since livestock no longer roamed in the area, it was proposed that the fence be donated for scrap. Governor Darden said the fence was not his to give away, although he mentioned that the "panel posts

...*because somebody talked!*

A wartime poster urging people to keep quiet about military matters. *National Archives.*

are heavy and are made in the form of fasces, the emblem of Fascist Italy." He also asserted "that when the White House donates its fence, we will discuss our Capitol Square fence." There was also resistance on the part of Richmond's leadership to the scrapping of Civil War artifacts. For example, the mayor said, "It would not be justifiable to turn over to the salvage committee the great iron anchor from the USS *Cumberland* that has been on the lawn of the White House of the Confederacy for decades." There was a major concern that some enthusiastic salvager might destroy irreplaceable relics when scrapping them was not really necessary. However, some Confederate cannonballs in Capitol Square were not considered irreplaceable and were relegated to the scrap heap.

The war, at this time, was being fought in Europe and in the Pacific, but censorship slowed up the information getting to the general public. The *Richmond News Leader* on September 12 commented that "Naval Censorship has reached the depths of absurdity. The public is being denied information to which it is entitled." For example, the Battle of Midway was fought and won by the United States in June 1942, but Richmonders did not learn until September 16, 1942, that the USS *Yorktown*, an aircraft carrier, was lost as a result of that battle. Much of the news was censored during the war, and there was a constant concern that someone might give away a military secret to a spy by careless comments. Slogans like "Loose Lips Sink Ships," "Free Speech Doesn't Mean Careless Talk" and "Button Your Lip" were posted throughout the community.

Although the losses of navy ships were well-kept military secrets, some military secrets were compromised in Richmond. The Navy Intelligence Office was in the city library building on Franklin Street and was a top-secret installation. However, on one windy day, officers and men were seen picking up every scrap of paper from the streets near the library building. Why were they doing this? The explanation was that in burning confidential papers, the navy had not counted on the up draft in the library furnace flues; thus, top-secret papers were being blown out of the chimney and scattered throughout the neighborhood. It could have been said that the navy's secrets were "Gone with the Wind."

Also passing away were old speed limit signs. In order to save gasoline and tires, the Virginia General Assembly reduced the state speed limit to thirty-five miles per hour. A quick check revealed that most trucks and buses were exceeding the new limit. They were stopped and fined accordingly. Since the goal was to save gas, many suggestions were made to get more miles to a gallon. One man claimed to get eighty-eight miles per gallon by following these rules: "drive no faster than 25 miles per hour; use first gear until the speed was at 15 miles per hour; and then shift to second; disconnect the automatic choke; never park your car in the sun since the sun can evaporate gas; keep the tires properly inflated; and coast down all hills." Apparently, there are no records to show if Richmonders used this system.

This news was followed by the launching of a three-week scrap drive running from September 21 to October 10, 1942. The drive, termed "Junk Rally Weeks," was sponsored by the newspapers of Virginia. The *Richmond News Leader*, in an editorial, commented, "This time the campaign is one that will require you to go down to your cellar and up to your attic for scrap that will be collected." It was pointed out that a wash pail could make three bayonets, an old radiator would make thirty rifles and an old teakettle could make eighty-four rifle cartridges. Soldiers from Camp Lee drove army trucks through Richmond to collect the scrap that had been placed in front yards or on the curb. But it was not long before enthusiasm for junk collection got out of control.

A group of boys picked up some newly delivered "railroad tie plates and spikes" and gave them to the scrap drive. The railroad promised to put future deliveries under guard. But one piece of railroad history was sacrificed. A solid brass hub cap from the driving wheel of the locomotive that took "Old 97" to glory in Danville, Virginia, was given away for scrap. In addition to railroad artifacts being donated, Richmonders were told that if their "automobiles were no longer suitable for transportation, they should be taken to a junk dealer."

Sanford Williamson and Walter Griggs in gas-saving vehicles. *Sanford Williamson Collection.*

After the scrap drive, a new proposal was made that was innovative in its effort to save gas and tires. A campaign was started to get pupils to walk to school. Although Dr. C.L. Outland, medical director for the Richmond Public Schools, felt walking students would be healthier, there was a problem. Parents were concerned about the safety of their children walking because they had to cross streets. Dr. Outland said that he understood the concerns of parents for the safety of their children crossing streets, but he suggested that because of the wartime regulations, there was not much traffic to worry about. He also encouraged teachers to walk to school. The plan was endorsed by the Richmond Police Department, which promised to look after the walking pupils. While walking was one way to save gas and tires, the post office discovered another way.

In September, the Richmond Post Office removed 303 mailboxes from neighborhoods to save more than 4,500 gallons of gasoline. In addition to removing the mailboxes, the post office started selling sheets for V-mail. V-mail consisted of a photographic process whereby a letter was written to a serviceman on a special V-Mail form that was then photographed on microfilm. The tiny negative was then rushed by bomber or ferry plane across the seas, enlarged for distribution and then given to the soldier or sailor in the war zone.

Like almost everything else, stoplights were also an issue. At the start of the war, traffic lights had V's and X's stenciled on them to make them invisible from the air during an air raid. Since this was not satisfactory, the stencils were removed, and transformers were installed to permit the lights to burn at sixty watts during the night or when there was a blackout. Another change was that the stoplights were adjusted so that the red signal was placed on the top and the green at the bottom in conformity with a national policy.

In late October, over four thousand Richmonders began to collect funds for the War and Community Fund Campaign. As if to emphasize the urgency of the campaign, there was an air-raid test with bombers flying over the city. The planes dropped "bombs" on Main Street and Broad Street Stations, the Telephone Building, the Power Company Building and the Richmond News Leader Building. It was also reported that "bombs" hit the yard of the Governor's Mansion, but the governor continued his work. Of course, this was all a drill, and the "bombs" contained two ounces of sand and a note stating the type of bomb dropped. It was not long before the Better Business Bureau had to warn Richmonders about a peddler going from door to door selling special sand that was supposed to put out fires from bombs immediately. However, it was only plain sand and nothing more. And things did not get better. Following the air raid, some 200 of Virginia Electric and Power Company's 463 bus operators went on a strike. The strike was a jurisdictional dispute between labor unions. Fortunately, the strike lasted only eleven hours, and there were enough nonstrikers to keep the transit system in operation. Any strike was seen as not supporting the servicemen in combat and generally did not get much public support.

Richmonders had been getting phone books for many years, but the ones distributed to telephone subscribers in 1942 were different. On each of the sixty-five thousand phone books was taped this message: "Please do not make telephone calls during or immediately after an air-raid alarm, as it is essential that the lines be kept free for use by the defense authorities. If your telephone rings, however, answer it promptly." It was also pointed out that telephone users should check their directories before calling "Information" for a number since more than half of such calls were for numbers listed in the directory.

On November 15, Richmonders' thoughts turned to the Pacific when President Roosevelt announced that "the turning point of the war has come." He called the victory at Guadalcanal a major victory for the United States. But the war was far from over, and there was an epitaph over a marine's grave in the Pacific that summed up the vicious island combat:

*And when he gets to heaven,*
*To St. Peter he will tell;*
*One more Marine reporting, sir—*
*I've served my time in hell.*

During the week of November 2, there was a major tin can drive. Large ads in the newspapers reported that city trucks would collect all tin cans. Richmonders were asked to do the following: remove the top and bottom from the can, take off the paper labels, wash the can, flatten it by crushing it with your foot and then put the cans in separate containers next to the regular trash. The ad was signed by the "Win With Tin Committee." In an effort to aid these efforts, Bing Crosby sang the best-forgotten song "Junk Ain't Junk Anymore 'Cause Junk Will Win the War." Other slogans included the following: "Slap the Jap with the Scrap" and "Hit Hitler with Junk." However, a correspondent to the *Richmond News Leader* wanted to know if "the government was getting all of the tin cans or were the beer brewers getting part of them." The concern was that those individuals in the temperance community did not want to be part of supporting breweries.

Richmond had supported the war in a variety of ways, but there was a problem in the city that was embarrassing. The United States was fighting a war against those who saw some people as unequal and inferior, and in Richmond, black schoolteachers made less money than their white counterparts. Seeking equal pay, the black teachers retained Oliver W. Hill, who would later rewrite history in 1954 in the school desegregation decision of *Brown v. the Board of Education*. Over time, adjustments were made to equalize the salaries. But there was another racial issue that seemed to always be in the news.

During the war, there were constant reports of the formation of "Eleanor Clubs," which were named after President Roosevelt's wife. These clubs may or may not have existed in Richmond. Their purpose was to discontinue the use of Negroes as servants, but other informants indicated that their purpose was to have servants dine with the families they served. Other alleged demands included the following: no colored maids in the kitchen by Christmas, no belittling of the president or his wife and the right to come through the front door instead of the back door. In addressing the issue, Governor Darden said that "he had received no authenticated reports of the prevalence of Eleanor Clubs in Virginia," and he said that he "was not concerned about the rumors surrounding their existence." The governor continued, "Most of the blame for racial uneasiness or propaganda are rumors without any basis in fact." He also said that he had been in contact with Negro leaders who had been most helpful. The governor was quoted in the Richmond newspapers as follows: "There has not been a word of truth in reports of organization of such clubs in Southern cities in which government agents have conducted their investigation." On a more positive note, it was pointed out that Negroes were participating in bond drives and would meet at the Mosque for a rally. The press noted that Negroes were willing to carpool with as many as eight people in a car, whereas whites were "selfish and wasteful for not carpooling."

While Richmond and the rest of America were dealing with racism, word started to filter out of Germany that Jews were being imprisoned, tortured and executed by the Nazis. Known as the "Final Solution," this action was characterized by gas chambers and death camps known by the infamous names of Auschwitz, Belzec, Bergen-Bergan and many more. For the civilized world, such mass executions were beyond comprehension, and for the Allied nations fighting the war, no firm action was taken to stop the slaughter until late in the war. Anne Frank, a young victim of the Holocaust, wrote these words of eternal hope, "Think of all the beauty still left around you and be happy."

There was a major rally at the Mosque on Armistice Day and a religious service at St. Paul's Episcopal Church. The rector of St. Paul's prayed that "we may wisely and reverently use our freedom." At the Mosque, war songs were sung, from "Over There" from World War I to "Praise the Lord and Pass the Ammunition." The theme at the Mosque rally was "What we need for victory."

Although "Praise the Lord and Pass the Ammunition" was sung, the song was not without controversy. The *Virginia Methodist Advocate* asked that the song be banned because it gave an erroneous conception of a chaplain's activities. Chaplains do not fire machine guns, and it was felt that the song might give our enemies the idea that chaplains were fighting, and they would be mistreated if captured. The argument might have been valid, but the song was not banned and continued to be near the top of the charts in popularity.

Richmonders celebrated a quiet Thanksgiving with many well-attended church services. Since restaurants were either filled with customers or closed, servicemen in the Richmond area were invited to eat with Richmond families. Unfortunately, a turkey might not have been on every table since many stores had run out of turkeys for the first time in recent memory. It was also unlikely that much coffee was served at Thanksgiving since it was now being rationed and was difficult to obtain. However, some people made coffee using acorns, grain, carrots, dandelions, potato peels or sweet potatoes.

Sweet potato coffee was used during the Civil War, and the recipe was printed in a Richmond newspaper so that it could be used in the current conflict. The recipe was as follows:

*Peel sweet potatoes and slice them three-quarters, or one half-inch thick, cut into strips the same width, the strips cut into squares so as to average the same size. Dry in the sun three days. When dry put into bags. When you use for coffee, parch a good brown, grind and make as you would coffee.*

Then there was major war news. The headline in the *Richmond Times-Dispatch* of November 8 reported, "U.S. Forces Invade French Africa." President Roosevelt felt that the invasion, known as Operation Torch, would give people in the United States a feeling that they were at war and let the Germans know that they would now have to face the United States. It also made names like Eisenhower, Patton and Rommel household words. At the same time, an evangelist came to Richmond and preached the sermon "Is Hitler the Beast?" at the Lyric Theatre.

Shortly after Thanksgiving, the Shore Patrol moved into Richmond to join the Military Police. These police units were needed to assist the Richmond police because, on the weekends, thousands of servicemen would come to Richmond to have a good time. To lessen some of the good times, the Shore Patrol put the Shockoe Valley District and the area north of Marshall Street between Adams and Tenth Streets out of bounds for navy personnel. However, there were still many places to have a good time and try to forget the war.

On December 7, 1942, "Remember Pearl Harbor" programs were held in the public schools. At Thomas Jefferson High School, members of the corps of cadets raised the "Stars and Stripes," while the cadet band played the national anthem. The entire student body stood at attention during the ceremony. Following the flag raising, a boy and a girl broadcasted special messages to the student body over the school's loudspeaker system, outlining what the average high school student could do to help win the war.

Not so patriotic was the disclosure in the *Richmond News Leader* that although federal offices were to have a maximum temperature of sixty-five degrees, most offices were in violation. Temperatures in some offices exceeded eighty degrees. The only place in full compliance with a temperature below seventy degrees was "an unheated hallway in the Post Office Building." At John Marshall High School, it was sixty-two degrees in a boys' washroom and seventy-eight degrees in the sunlit library of Thomas Jefferson High School. Federal authorities asked the public to keep their houses at temperatures between sixty-five and seventy degrees. A survey revealed that most homeowners were in compliance.

As Christmas drew closer, it was announced that for the first time in nineteen years, Richmond would not have a community Christmas pageant. It was reported that "the story of the nativity, which has been held annually in tableaux on a stage in Capitol Square at dusk on Christmas Eve, would not be presented this year due to a shortage of man power." It was also reported that Richmond would not have a community Christmas tree. However, bookstores reported that the Bible remained the bestselling book and a popular Christmas present.

Christmas would not be so merry for chickens and goats in Richmond because they might become someone's meal. It was discovered that the city code did not prohibit a person from keeping a few chickens, providing the rooster did not crow so loudly that he became a nuisance. (My grandfather was visited by the police for having a crowing rooster in the backyard.) You could also keep a goat, but you needed to buy a license. However, no one seemed to want a goat since no goat licenses had been sold in years. In a note of humor, a reporter wrote, "It is possible that the FBI might get after you, if you keep a goat, on the charge that you are sabotaging the war effort because the goats eat tin cans and tin is essential to the war effort." The city code did not prohibit the keeping of a horse or a cow in your yard. It was even reported that a person could keep pigeons but not pigs. Pigs were banned from backyards in 1899.

Books read during the war, including a nurse's New Testament. *Author's collection.*

A toy truck typical of the toys given at Christmas. *Author's collection.*

A few days before Christmas, Richmond churches listed their Christmas services in great detail. Some of the sermon titles included the following: "Christmas Has a New Meaning," "The Gift that Transformed the World," "The Prince of Peace," "Can the Angel Song be True" and "How Far Is It to Bethlehem." Many churches planned special music. Mount Olivet played "Heavenly Music" and Union Station Methodist planned "An Hour of Anthems and Carols," while Laurel Street Methodist's Cherub Choir sang, "For Our Lord."

In addition to the announcement of Christmas programs, it was reported that stores were virtually sold out of Christmas presents, trees and candy. Traditional toys like rubber balls, tricycles and doll carriages were gone. About the only toys available were crude wooden gadgets and some secondhand toys. It was also reported that liquor store shelves were about empty. It can be assumed that Richmond's bootlegging community was making money.

More in the true spirit of Christmas was something that happened on Broad Street. About seventy-five Christmas shoppers were waiting for a streetcar, but all of the streetcars were already full and passed the waiting shoppers without stopping. Then, Mrs. A.M. Flippen suggested that all the waiting passengers sing Christmas carols. Soon, the streetcar-waiting choir started singing everything from "Silent Night" to "Jingle Bells." Although they probably sang "White Christmas," Richmonders were disappointed that a promised white Christmas had melted away before the big day and was replaced with a fog so heavy that it was difficult to see the Cathedral of the Sacred Heart from Monroe Park.

On Christmas day, the local papers were filled with messages of Christmas. One of the happiest was that the "Christmas Mother Fund had gone over the top and once again many children would get presents that otherwise they could not afford." One writer pleaded, "Whatever the form of your Christmas service may be—churchgoing, meditation, carol singing, a quiet hour by the fireside with your family, a visit to an old friend—please include one thing: a letter to some man in the armed services." It was suggested that these letters should contain cheerful news and what was being done at home to strengthen the fighting front.

Jay Franklin, in his column "We the People," wrote "that we should remember the war for freedom and the shift away from the spirit of materialism, which marked a new note in our national point of view." He continued, "In recent years, it was difficult to detect whether Christmas in America was a religious festival or a nationwide sales campaign. It was true that the churches were crowded on Christmas Day, but it was also true that the department stores were crowded for a month before Christmas." He then continued with this thought:

> *In 1942, a new kind of Christmas gift was on the market. You could get it anywhere, except across the shop counter. You could not wear it and nobody could wrap it. That gift is the life-blood of brave men.*

He then summarized his thoughts:

> *Some servicemen are going down in the oceans, some are dying of cold or hunger, flame or shell. But they are giving their all in order that the world might find its way through this time of evil and darkness. What Lincoln called "the last full measure of devotion" is the Christmas gift of 1942.*

Many local businesses placed ads in the paper thanking their customers for their patronage. Some of these businesses were as follows: Hudson Brothers; Chiocca and Sons; B.A. Cephas; Powell Brothers; Home Furniture Store; J.A. Black Sons, Inc., Furniture; Ever-Ready Transfer; Richmond Sand and Gravel Corp; Friedman's Loan Office; and The Nook.

With a rather austere Christmas but a memory, war stories were again in the newspapers, along with developments in the Richmond area. The Quartermaster Depot at Bellwood was reporting that all transportation would be nearly "100 percent horse-and-buggy-age style with some World War I equipment as part of the participating rolling stock." Before long, "Gee" and "Haw" were heard on the post, along with "Forward, march." The commanding officer conceded "that horse-drawn wagons were slower, but they are sure and require less overseeing and repairs."

As Richmonders celebrated a quiet New Year's Eve, they could reflect on a year that had changed the lives of just about everyone. The list included changes in transportation, speed limits, food costs and the cost of living. But these changes were mere inconveniences compared to the fifty-nine Richmond servicemen who were either dead or missing in action. The year 1942 was one when Richmonders were thrown into a new world, a world of death and destruction. But the year that had begun in the oily, dark smoke of Pearl Harbor was now beginning to see the sunlight stream through the dark clouds of war, even as oil continued to bubble up from the hulk of the USS *Arizona* from its grave in the mud at Pearl Harbor.

# CHAPTER 5

# KEEP HIM FLYING,
# BUY WAR BONDS, 1943

*One of our planes was missing*
*Two hours overdue*
*One of our planes was missing*
*With all its gallant crew*
*The radio sets were humming*
*We waited for a word*
*Then a noise broke*
*Through the humming and this is what we heard*

*Comin' in on a wing and a prayer*
*Comin' in on a wing and a prayer*
*Though there's one motor gone*
*We can still carry on*
*Comin' in on a wing and a prayer.*
—*Harold Adamson and Jimmie McHugh*

There is nothing routine about fighting a world war, and there is nothing routine about life on the homefront. However, this war had been going on for over a year, and Richmonders seemed to be getting used to it, if you can ever get used to having your loved ones killed and your life changed forever.

During 1943, rationing was tightened, blackouts and air raids became more frequent, more traffic restrictions were put in place and penalties for the violation of regulations were more severe. Especially annoying was that sliced bread was no longer available, so there was a run on bread knives. Unfortunately, bread knives were scarce, and those housewives without them complained that they could not cut the bread thin enough with regular knives to put it in their toasters. There were other complaints that focused on government programs and regulations that many people felt had become irksome. But the *Richmond Times-Dispatch* asserted that "compared with the soldier, the civilian continued to live in the lap of luxury." The lap of luxury, however, did not include pleasure driving.

In January, all pleasure driving was forbidden. Social calls and travel to amusements parks by automobile were forbidden. Enforcement of the pleasure driving regulation was demonstrated when a well-known Richmond accountant was prosecuted for taking his family to dinner at the Country Club of Virginia. Another man was cited for driving one block out of his way on legitimate business, and still another driver was issued a summons for driving two blocks out of his way to find a parking space. Cars were not the only problem. Streetcars and buses continued to be packed with people. Taxicabs did not seem to be an option. One Richmonder commented, "You would have to be near death if you had hope of getting a taxi." But public transportation was more than a nuisance. There were concerns that segregation on public transportation vehicles might spark a race riot.

Buses and streetcars were jammed with people, and blacks had to wade through a "mass of tired, sweating, and irritable white people standing in the aisle in the front of the bus to get to the back of the bus or streetcar," where Virginia state law required them to sit. The acting police chief said, "Northern black soldiers and sailors deliberately took front seats on cars and buses" to create problems. In view of the chaotic conditions of public transportation, many Richmonders supported desegregation on public conveyances, but it did not happen. Richmond remained a racially segregated city fighting a world war against racism. The *Richmond News Leader* reported that Catherine Jones Coleman, a black woman, refused to move and occupy a rear seat on a Richmond bus. The judge said, "Offenses of this type are getting entirely too numerous. Negro people and white people have lived harmoniously together in Richmond for many years. I have no intention of letting this law be violated and thus bringing on further trouble. I am going to go right on enforcing it." But segregation on mass transportation was only part of the problem. There were times when black soldiers were treated like second-class citizens in Richmond.

A black soldier, who was very tired and worn out from a long train ride, went into the USO lounge, where a white hostess told him that the lounge

The USO building used by black servicemen. The exterior has been somewhat altered since the war. *Photograph by Walter Griggs.*

was only for white soldiers. Someone observed the event and wrote, "When the evicted soldier looked toward the USO sign, he had tears in his eyes." After looking at the sign for some time, he lamented, "This is what I get for being a soldier." There was a USO facility for blacks, but it was generally filled with "white taxicab drivers hanging out, chewing, smoking, and spitting on the floor."

It takes a real person to fight for a nation that can afford him nothing better than a spit-covered floor and a dirty table at which to eat. On another occasion in Richmond, a white man commented, "When this war is over we are going to put you n-----s back in your place." A second white man indignantly responded, "These guys are fighting to keep you out of the fire and you are sitting at home figuring how to put them back into their places when the war is over." The irate speaker continued, "My guess is you won't be here when the war is over." And Governor Darden did not help matters by commenting, "Colored people would have been better off if the South had won the Civil War."

This was not the only case of racism in this area. One lady wrote a letter to the newspaper in which she said that she was in a physician's waiting room when a black soldier came in and sat down. A nurse told him he had to leave the waiting room and stand in the hall. The white woman and her sick son left the waiting room and stood with the soldier, whom she learned had volunteered to serve in the army over a year earlier.

Efforts to provide help for Richmond's black citizens failed when the school superintendent refused to hire a black assistant to aid in promoting education for blacks. He also denied admission to a black student to the Virginia Mechanics Institute. The superintendent commented, "I do not think it is practical to admit Negro boys to the Mechanics Institute at the present time." The situation did not get any better when a black girl wanted to take a test at a white school. Permission was refused with the comment that "we have schools for Negroes."

Armstrong Colored High School was the first public school in Richmond for black students. It lacked many needed resources, including a gymnasium. When parents asked for a mat to put on the floor in the makeshift gymnasium, the white principal refused to approve it. It was not long before a girl fell and broke her arm. Parents were rightfully upset. They also wanted a black principal to lead a black school. The irate parents pointed out that the current principal had not attended a PTA meeting in over eight years. In contrast, Maggie L. Walker, the other high school for blacks, was a beautiful building and a state-of-the-art educational institution. Described as "a keystone in the arch of Richmond's educational system," its first class graduated in 1942.

Richmond had another crisis on January 27. The city was hit with its worst sleet storm in more than fifty years, and damage to trees was catastrophic. By one count, seventy-five thousand trees were damaged. Because of falling trees breaking power lines, many homes and businesses lost power and telephone service. In the Stewart Station Post Office on Broad Street,

The old Armstrong Colored High School as it appeared in 2013. *Photograph by Walter Griggs.*

workers sorted the mail by candlelight, and most families lit their homes by candlelight or old oil lamps.

But one thing that not even a sleet storm could stop was the induction of men into the military. In the early days of the war, the Richmond Induction Center was in the Blues Armory. Then the center was moved to the Belgium Building on the campus of Virginia Union University. That building had been built for Belgium and was part of the New York World's Fair of 1939. When the Nazis took over Belgium, the building could not be sent back, so it was gifted to Virginia Union University. The new induction center was described as the "swankiest" induction center in the United States.

If you were not inducted into the service, you were faced with a shoe problem. The media reported that shoes would be rationed and that shoes for both men and women would be very plain. Women's shoes would be available in only four colors, and banned were leather frills, fancy overlaps, bows and leather laces. Shoes were also mentioned in a story about a Japanese flag that was kept on the floor in front of an officer's desk at the Richmond Air Base.

The Belgium Building on the campus of Virginia Union University that served as an induction center during the war. *Photograph by Walter Griggs.*

Whenever someone stepped up to the desk, he would wipe his shoes on the flag.

In addition to shoe rationing, it was also reported that new alarm clocks were no longer available; therefore, it was important to take care of the one you owned. According to one survey, seventeen thousand Richmonders were waiting for a war model clock that was described as an "ugly duckling" model. One buyer said, "It was a hideous-looking excuse for a clock." She said that the "clock was made largely of plastic, cardboard and other nondefense materials but was guaranteed to do a faithful job signaling the arrival of a new day with a loud and unpleasant ringing."

In early 1943, War Production Regulation L85 was issued, requiring changes to save cloth by defining the kinds of clothes men and women could buy. For women, new regulations affected every kind of clothing produced in America, except wedding gowns, maternity clothes, infant wear and religious vestments. The order stipulated that only one and three-quarters yards of fabric could be used per dress. To meet this standard, women's hemlines were shortened, blouses were made without cuffs and had only one pocket and sashes were not permitted. A major problem was the lack of nylon hose for women. Since hose were not available, cosmetic companies developed leg makeup to make legs look like they were covered by stockings. Some of the names for this makeup included the following: Velva Leg Film, DuBarry Leg Make-up, Liquid Leg, Leg Shaw, Stockingless Cream and Leg Charm. In order to save money, some women stained their legs with tea. In addition to leg makeup, many women used eyebrow pencils to draw seams up the back of their legs. Max Factor marketed a device to help make the line straight.

These new dress restrictions also created the two-piece bathing suit for women in order to save cloth. Although women accepted the two-piece bathing suit for the summer, they were concerned that exposed knees, caused by shorter dresses, would cause their owners to catch cold in the winter. A panel of Richmond physicians advised women that they would not catch a cold by not covering their knees. Ironically, many Richmonders got sick in late winter with colds and the grippe. But the physicians believed it came from riding on crowded, public transportation vehicles and not from cold knees. As a practical matter, more and more women were wearing pants as they entered the workplace, and pants became a sign of patriotism. They identified a woman as working to support the troops.

Men's clothing restrictions continued with more specific regulations. Men could buy only single-breasted suits with pants without pleats or cuffs. There was also a movement for men to stop removing their hats in elevators. Since elevators in the 1940s were controlled by an operator who could not move the elevator until everyone was safely inside, not removing a hat could save time. The movement gained some support.

It seemed during the war that if one problem was solved, another one surfaced. For example, the Methodists were upset when they learned that liquor stores could stay open six days a week, but "our churches must be closed six days a week because of fuel shortages. Even the Sunday night services changed to afternoon to conserve the fuel supply, but liquor stores are open and heated six days a week." The Methodists continued to lobby against the sale of spirits that were not spiritual.

Richmonders did not know it, but an act of courage, sacrifice and faith was taking place in the icy North Atlantic. The USAT *Dorchester* was torpedoed by a German U-boat and began to sink. On board the ship were four chaplains: Methodist minister George L. Fox, Rabbi Alexander D. Goode, Roman Catholic priest John P. Washington and Reformed Church in America minister Clark V. Poling. When the supply of life jackets ran out, the four chaplains removed their own life jackets and gave them to others so they would have a chance to survive. As the *Dorchester* slipped beneath the waves, the four chaplains could be seen standing with their arms linked together saying these prayers: "*Sh'ma Yis'ra'eil Adonai Eloheinu Adonai echad.*" [Hear, Israel, the Lord is our God, the Lord is One] and "Our Father, which art in Heaven, Hallowed be Thy name. Thy Kingdom come, Thy will be done…"

The death of the four chaplains in the Atlantic Ocean was followed by another tragedy that occurred in the Pacific Ocean in the Naval Battle of Guadalcanal. The *Richmond Times-Dispatch* reported, "Five Sullivan Boys, All Missing, Got Chance They Asked For." At their request, the five Sullivan brothers of Waterloo, Iowa, were all serving together on the USS *Juneau* when the light cruiser was torpedoed and sunk. None of the five brothers survived. Their mother could only say through her tears, "But if they are gone, it will be some comfort to know they went together—as they wanted—and gave their lives for their country and victory." How does a family deal with the loss of their five sons? Mrs. Sullivan could only repeat what her boys would write in their letters, "Keep your chin up."

While heroes were dying, men and women were suffering in the Richmond city jail. It was reported that the prisoners "subsisted primarily on a diet of molasses, meal, soup and cabbage; that three dogs were kept in the jail to kill the rats which ran everywhere; that vermin and lice infested the bedding; and that women prisoners were locked up in the attic with poor ventilation and an unbelievable lack of privacy." Richmonders found little comfort in being told that it was not the worst jail in the state. Once the sorry state of the jail was made public, improvements were made almost immediately.

Equally disgusting was the surging prostitution rate in Richmond involving girls as young as twelve. Medical facilities for them were so overcrowded that many of the girls were kept in jail until appropriate treatment could be arranged. Also causing problems were students who were not attending school. The general reason for not attending was, according to one delinquent scholar, that "boys ain't thinking about anything these days but working and making money." The chief attendance officer for the Richmond Public Schools had an impossible job.

As a war measure, most Richmond restaurants started closing one day each week because of food shortages, too many customers and the scarcity of waitresses, who had found better jobs in the factories. Some of the restaurants that closed once a week were the following: Daley's, the Occidental, Elmore's, Bob's Seafood Grill, Wakefield Grill, Byrd Delicatessen, New York Delicatessen, Ewart's and Langford's. For Richmonders who liked to dine out, they were advised that there was no relief in sight. Whereas restaurants could close, school cafeterias had to stay open to provide food for the students, but they were running short of meat. To fill in the gap, meat alternatives were used, including peanut butter, dried beans, peas, eggs, cheese and milk. Although the lack of meat did not seem to concern students, they were very upset when they could have ice cream only once a week.

To continue to finance the war, there was another bond drive. To encourage donations, a Japanese submarine involved in the attack on Pearl Harbor was placed in front of the Miller and Rhoads Department Store on Broad Street. Ironically, a woman who worked in the store had been in Hawaii on December 7 and last saw the submarine on a beach. Anyone could see the interior of the submarine by buying a dollar's worth of War Savings Stamps. Children could peek inside with the purchase of twenty-five cents' worth of the stamps.

Easter 1943 was celebrated with the traditional Sunrise Services, which were held in various locations, including Capitol Square, Bryan Park and Chimborazo Park. Following these early services, many Richmonders attended Easter church services at 11:00 a.m. Sermon topics at the various churches included: "A Risen Christ," "Easter Love," "Discovery at the Dawn," "A New Interpretation of Easter" and "Easter Joy in a World at War." The newspapers reported that every church was packed, and many churches had to place chairs in the aisles to handle the overflow. Following the services and a midday meal, thousands of people joined in the Easter Parade, including many people in uniform. Unfortunately for the children, candy bunnies and chocolate eggs were ruled out by the War Production Board.

To keep churches full following Easter, the Richmond Ministerial Union placed posters in all nearby military camps listing the addresses of the churches in the area and inviting servicemen to attend. Attendance did remain high, but there was some question about whether it was because of a need for spiritual growth or the fact that the USO started a program where young women would attend church with soldiers or sailors. A sign at the USO on Grace Street stated, "If you want to go to heaven, go to church with an angel"—the angel being a young woman.

Some of those who attended church "with an angel" were assigned to the navy's V-12 Program, which was offered on the campus of the University of Richmond. The program was designed to train U.S. Navy and Marine Corps officers. Beginning on July 1, 1943, these trainees lived on campus in Thomas Hall and Jeter Hall and participated in all aspects of campus life. They took a seventeen-hour academic course load per semester, along with physical conditioning. This was a very successful program for the navy while providing needed students for the university to replace those who had left to join the armed forces.

While officers were being trained for combat, some Richmonders wrote letters to the *Richmond News Leader* focusing on several issues. One series of letters dealt with Richmond's hospitality toward visitors. One letter described "Richmond as a city with a star-spangled heart, for its streets are thick with men in uniform and its shop windows echo the patriotism of the homefront." One soldier liked the "ringing of great bells in the church steeples that pointed to the sky." A number of soldiers wrote to the newspaper and commented about the hospitality they found in Richmond. Another soldier wrote, "I have never felt as homesick as I did, since I came to Virginia. Evidently, the person who wrote the song 'Carry Me Back to Old Virginia [*sic*]' meant it literally as the only time anybody will be able to get a visitor back here is by having him carried here forcibly, or in a pine box." A Richmond soldier declared that his "home city [Richmond] was the most inhospitable one that he had seen." Another soldier commented that "Sunday in Richmond is touched with Southern magic. No whiskey bars, but bootleggers do a rousing business under the nose of the law." (Well, not always. One bootlegger was arrested twice on the same day. He told the judge, "I am going to Petersburg to sell whiskey.")

Church bells and religious celebrations seemed to have little impact on one Richmonder's attitude toward soldiers who visited Richmond from north of the Mason-Dixon line. A correspondent wrote to the *Richmond News Leader*:

> *All I can say is, I think these "damn Yankees," as they were called back in Civil War days, are still "damn Yankees." A soldier asked me why Richmonders say "aboot" for "about." I told him the people I associate with do not say "aboot." I then heard some foreigners (as I call Yankees) talking—it sounded like a cat and dog fight—some talking through their noses, others making sounds that could not be understood by the average person.*

For some Richmonders, the Civil War was not over, and Yankees were not wanted even if they were fighting to save the republic.

Of course, it did not take long for another letter to be printed in the paper. A person who signed a letter "By By Blues" commented on the southern pronunciation of "goodbye." She asserted that in "Richmond people say "Goodbah or goo' ba-a-a." She then explained that the "a" has a very flat, nasal sound somewhat similar to the "a" in "hat." Then she pointed out that "by" is pronounced "buy." Not content with one broadside attack, the writer continued by stating, "There are times when the air is split with sounds strangely reminiscent of the bleating of a flock of sheep: 'B-a-a' 'B-a-a-a-h' 'G'b-a-a.'" She then urged that Richmonders give the "heave-ho to 'Goo-ba-a-a.'"

After discussing civility, the Civil War and language in the newspapers, attention turned to women who were holding nontraditional jobs. Since more and more women were driving taxicabs in Richmond, there were a number of articles about them. One female cabdriver commented that "most of the Army and Navy men are full of fun and are usually good tippers." She continued that "soldiers are nearly always gay [funny] and keep me laughing, but I have never had one to be fresh." However, she did admit that she once picked up an elderly man who pushed his foot down as if to put on the brake each time the cabdriver did the same thing. Finally, the passenger said, "Don't mind me, it is just a habit." This same female cabdriver probably upset some women when she commented that "most women are very poor drivers since they have little regard for traffic rules." Richmonders could comment on cabdrivers, but their minds were never far from the grim reality of the war.

Virtually every day, the newspapers carried a notice of the death, wounding or capture of Richmonders accompanied by pictures. Typical was the announcement of the death of Second Lieutenant Sidney Warner Ironmonger Jr. of the U.S. Army Air Force. The lieutenant was a graduate of Thomas Jefferson High School and later attended the University of Virginia. He had left the university in his third year to enter the army air force. He died in a plane accident in the Pacific Theater. (When I was a student at Thomas Jefferson, I saw his name on a plaque in the hall, and I once heard a teacher comment about him.) Although the death of Americans brought great sadness, this was not the case in the deaths of enemy soldiers.

The May 15 edition of the *Richmond News Leader* carried a major news story. Admiral Isoroku Yamamoto, the commander in chief of the Pearl Harbor attack, had been killed by United States forces. In an editorial, the comment was made that "Yamamoto was an example of the arrogant spirit that most arouses the fighting blood of this nation." It was pointed out that he once said that "he would dictate peace terms to the United States in the White House." This did not happen. Later, it was revealed that he was ambushed and shot down in aerial combat.

In July, United States forces landed in Sicily, and on July 26, it was announced that Mussolini had quit. This pleased a lot of Richmonders, including the Italian Americans. In what might seem to be an uncharacteristically harsh letter, a minister wrote the following to the *Richmond Times-Dispatch*, "Could his highness Pope Pius XII turn over Mussolini to the Allies in exchange for not bombing Rome? Why not have the Allies then turn over Il Duce [Mussolini] to the Ethiopians for a daily diet of one pint of castor oil such as he gave to his political opponents?" The United States did not take his advice, but the days of Mussolini were about to end.

One of the few stories about Richmond during the war to appear in the national media was that of the Tredegar Iron Works, which appeared in the *Saturday Evening Post* in 1943. The article focused on the fact that the company made cannons for Generals Robert E. Lee and Thomas J. "Stonewall" Jackson, as well as munitions for World War II. The story commented on the advanced age of most of the workers, its rich heritage and the excellence of its products. The company office had only one telephone, which was in a phone booth. When the president of the company got a call, he would walk fifty feet to the phone booth to talk to the caller. It was also noted that the president opened all the mail so that he could be kept aware of what was going on. When asked why the company did things in such an old-fashioned way, the response was: "We have always done it that way." Considering its excellent production record, which was recognized by the armed forces, perhaps there was no reason to change.

As happened on a regular basis, there was another bond drive at the Mosque that featured appearances by Bob Hope, Jerry Colonna and Fred Astaire. Fred Astaire commented, "Southern girls have natural rhythm which makes them better dancing pupils." Dancing was also in the news when Camp Peary instituted a requirement that hose must be worn at the Camp Peary Service Club. As a result, "the Richmond girls, now accustomed to going bare-legged, refused to attend the function." Dancing remained in the news when it was announced that the Thalhimers' Parking Lot at Seventh and Grace Streets was being converted into a dance pavilion during the summer months to provide an additional place for the servicemen who came to Richmond every weekend to dance and party. The downtown facility was called the "Parking Lot Canteen for Dancing Under the Stars." Other dances were held at the Mosque, Monroe Center, the Knights of Columbus building, the Jewish Social Center and the YMCA.

Unfortunately, the good times were frequently followed by bad times. There were persistent rumors that a race riot would take place in Richmond on July 4. Several months earlier, a letter carrier had been asked by government officials if he knew of any riot plans by blacks. The man said that he knew of no such plans. In another case, a black man told a white man that he was not aware of any plans for a riot. Although both black men denied that they had heard of any such plans, there were persistent stories that blacks were buying ice picks to use as weapons. Then an African American newspaper did a survey of 100 black citizens from all walks of life, and none had heard of any riot plans. But a black writer wrote, "Whites fear a riot because they know that colored people have been mistreated to the point of rioting." The Black Ministers' Conference believed enemy agents were starting the rumors. The truth of the matter was that no riot had been planned, but Richmond police were on the alert. However, a black family's home in Oregon Hill was stoned by a gang of 250 whites. They did not want a black family living in a predominately white neighborhood. Unfortunately, race riots took place in July in Detroit and other cities, and the Axis powers quickly let their people know about racial unrest in the United States.

Following the threat of unrest, Richmond had to deal with another problem. In mid-summer, a squirrel jumped on a person who was walking down the street. Immediately, the papers reported that some people wanted to "do away with some of the city's bushy nut-eaters by shooting them." Then a counter drive started to protect our fuzzy friends with the sharp teeth. The supporters of the squirrels were those Richmonders who frequented the "primitive wilds of Monroe Park" and who "seemed willing to fight for the last peanut for their friends." Once the squirrel problem was solved, another animal started to smell. It seems that a skunk had started "smelling out" near the State Capitol. To the relief of everyone, the skunk was finally seen strolling down Grace Street toward the West End with its tail held high. Experts suggested that the skunk was in Capitol Square looking for a "government handout."

While some people were fighting to save the animals, others were fighting to save their jalopies (old, worn-out cars like the Corvair I had in college). Because of the wartime shortage of new cars, owners had to keep their old cars, which some residents felt was a blight on the landscape. A movement that started in Pennsylvania wanted people to junk their jalopies and viewed driving one as unpatriotic. A group of Richmonders called this movement an "unfair discrimination against owners of jalopies." To protect the right to drive a jalopy, the "Jalopy Owners Mutual Protective Association of America, Inc." was organized in Richmond. The group claimed that there were more than thirty thousand cars in the United States over seven years old, and the rights of those cars and their owners needed to be protected.

Saving jalopies was considered positive by many people, but selling scrap from a battlefield raised some questions. Two railroad carloads of salvaged war material from the North African Campaign arrived in Richmond and were sent to the Smith Junk and Salvage Company. There were over fifty tons of plane parts, motorcycles, helmets, tank treads, armor plate and gasoline containers from Nazi tanks abandoned in the desert. Many Richmonders rushed to the junkyard to get souvenirs of the war. It was reported that someone took two Italian machine guns. But the sale of the scrap raised some issues. In a letter to a newspaper editor, a sailor asked this question: "How much in blood did the scrap cost us? And who will be the one who profits the most from this deal between the Eastern broker and the Richmond junkman? I wonder what the Virginia boys who are fighting will think when they read in the *Richmond News Leader* that some guy is making a profit in theirs and their buddies' blood." His concerns were not addressed.

Even though there was a war, there was still time for a beauty contest. The Miss Richmond Contest took place in September and offered a diversion from the war, endless scrap drives and fundraising events. The Hotel John Marshall was the scene of the pageant, which had fifteen contestants. The judges were headed by Harry Conover, director of a famed New York modeling agency. Prior to the contest, Mr. Conover said, "It is hard to top the Southern girls' natural, well-scrubbed beauty." Dorothy Taylor, a student at the Pan American School, was named Miss Richmond and represented Richmond in the Miss America Contest in Atlantic City. Upon her return to Richmond, it was reported that she and the other contestants for Miss America had sold over $1,000,000 in War Bonds.

While beauty contestants were selling bonds, Richmond school students were learning a new way to salute the flag. Schoolchildren had been taught that the flag salute was an outstretched arm pointed at the flag. This was now similar to the salute used by Nazi Germany. To clearly separate themselves from Hitler and his Nazis, public school children in Richmond were told that the "salute would now be holding the right hand over the heart." The students also repeated the "Pledge of Allegiance" every day. The comment was made that "Richmond boys and girls engaged in total war against the followers of the hooked cross repeat their allegiance daily with new understanding regardless of the system of homage they follow—outstretched arm or hand over heart."

Blackouts continued in 1943, although it became increasingly apparent that Richmond would not be bombarded from the sea or bombed from the air. Children of the war years can still recall the blackouts. Frances recalls the heavy shades that were placed at every window, and she was admonished when she tried to peep under them. Ruth can still remember sitting in the dark on her mother's lap while watching the circle of light on the radio that helped one to find a station in the dark. Most families listened to the radio to get information about the blackout. Clint can still recall a frightening experience that his family had. They had just built a fire in the fireplace when the sirens signaled a blackout. In a few minutes, there was a rapping on the door as his family waited in the dark. When the door was opened, the

Monkey, bear and doll—toys belonging to Frances and Walter Griggs. Please note the lack of hair on the bear and the monkey. *Frances and Walter Griggs Collection.*

air-raid warden told his family that he could see the light from the fireplace in the dark. His parents then held a blanket in front of the fireplace to make sure no light could be seen. Carolyn remembers sitting in the living room with her mother with all of the curtains drawn and with only one little blue light bulb providing light. While she waited with her mother, her father patrolled with the Auxiliary Police. Joan recalls her mother making a party out of blackouts by serving cereal to keep her occupied while her father was walking the streets serving as an air-raid warden. My own experience was a little different. I recall being told to lie on the floor and keep quiet. But to stay calm, I pulled the hair out of my stuffed monkey and bear. After the war, they were a sorry sight.

Jill, who lived outside of London, felt the impact of the air raids in a different way since England was being bombed on a regular basis. Her family built a bomb shelter in the backyard; and in a room in her house, her family kept their gasmasks. And unlike Richmonders, she saw the glass windows shattering from nearby bomb blasts. Her greatest fear was the German rockets, which the Germans called V1s or "hell hounds" and Jill called "doodlebugs." Launched from France, no one knew where they might hit. One "doodlebug" hit London's Tower Bridge. The one thing all people who were young during the war seem to remember is the blackouts—whether they were just a precaution or for real.

On September 9, there was good news. The headline in the *Richmond Times-Dispatch* stated, "Allied Units Land in Naples Area after Full Capitulation of Italy." Additional stories reported that Germany felt betrayed by the Italians. Richmond Italians rejoiced over the fall of their homeland to the Allied powers. Later, Italy declared war on Germany. The nation that President Roosevelt said had stabbed "a dagger in the back of its neighbor" now stabbed a dagger into the back of its former ally.

Labor Day was not celebrated, but Richmonders were able to enjoy the benefits of the removal of the pleasure-driving restrictions on travel. People were "pouring into theater parking lots, nightclubs, and parks; and hunters were able to drive their cars to find a place to hunt ducks, geese or quail." But the removal of restrictions on pleasure driving did not change the need to raise money to fight the war.

War Bonds were for sale at the Merrimac on Broad Street. But this time, there was a special marketing effort. The Navy Mother's Club was able to borrow a torpedo from the navy for bond buyers to sign. One man bought $100 worth of bonds and promptly signed his name on the lethal weapon. It was pointed out that if one wanted to send a message to Japan by "torpedo mail," this was the chance to do it. The plan was for the autographed torpedo to be delivered by a submarine, a destroyer or a PT boat to a ship flying the flag of the "Land of the Rising Sun."

To deliver mail in a more conventional fashion, the post office requested that Richmonders use postal zone numbers when they wrote to family and friends in the city. The reason for the request was that the postal workers who were new and inexperienced would be able to move the mail more swiftly if they had zone numbers. Some of the zone numbers were as follows: West of the Boulevard was zone 21, anywhere on the Northside was zone 22 and South Side was zone 24. The postmaster's office also suggested that "packages for servicemen be wrapped and packed in newspaper since the boys will read every word in a hometown paper, advertisements and all, no matter how old the paper."

As part of the war effort on the homefront, every week or so the *Richmond News Leader* would publish a column labeled "Week's OCD [Office of Civil Defense] News." Some of the events for September were as follows:

> *Canning—OCD canning classes given in co-operation with the Adult Education Department of the Richmond Public Schools will be held this week.*
>
> *Training Classes—A class in gas defense will be held at the John Marshall High School auditorium.*
>
> *Defense Science Unit—Girls registered with the Chaperones' Club will attend dances at Camp Lee this week.*

During World War II, planes were frequently given names by their crews, as well as having pictures painted on them. Names and pictures could turn an ordinary aircraft into something special and personal for the crew. One such plane was a B-17 Flying Fortress named June Bug, and it had a painted June bug on the nose. This was a special name since it was believed to be the first B-17 named after a Richmond woman. The woman was June McClure Jeter, whose husband was Lieutenant Sydney Jeter, the pilot of the plane. Mrs. Jeter told her parents that it was one of only two decent names on planes in the squadron. Mrs. Jeter did not consider names like Burpin' Buzzard, Passionate Witch, The Moose or Tailwind acceptable names.

Charles Nance Major was born in Richmond and later commissioned an ensign in the United States Navy. He was killed in action in the North Atlantic while serving aboard the SS *R.P. Resor*, a tanker owned by Standard Oil, which was sunk by *U-578* of the German Navy. On October 23, 1943, history was made when, for the first time in naval history, a naval officer christened a navy ship. Ensign Margaret Roper Major, the widow of Ensign Charles Major, christened the USS *Major*, a destroyer escort, at a shipyard in Orange, Texas. The USS *Major* served throughout the war and was present at the Japanese surrender in Tokyo Bay.

Another Richmonder honored for heroism by having a navy destroyer escort named in his honor was Edward Max Price, who graduated from the United States Naval Academy. He was assigned to the USS *Lexington* and

The blessing of the crew of a B-17 before taking off for a bomb run over Germany. *National Archives.*

died in the Battle of the Coral Sea. The USS *Price* was christened by his mother, Mrs. R.P. Reynolds, at the Orange, Texas shipyard.

Then a controversy developed. Wartime censorship had precluded pictures of dead Americans. The only pictures of combat casualties showed the bodies covered. This changed in September 1943, when pictures of dead Americans lying on Buna Beach, Papua, New Guinea, were published. President Roosevelt believed that the American people might have grown complacent about the horrors of war and supported the publication of the pictures. Seeing Americans lying dead with their contorted bodies on the sand in front of a destroyed landing craft brought people back to reality. There was a general consensus that these pictures helped people realize the tragedy and sacrifices of war.

In late October, there was a tragedy at St. Philips Hospital for Negroes. A rat slithered into the nursery and bit two infants, and one of them died. The hospital director admitted "that rats have been prevalent for many months and about eighty have been killed by hospital personnel." Richmonders were shocked, and a cleanup was demanded. Steps were taken to alleviate the rat problem, but the thought of rats running around an infant nursery upset the entire community, as did a similar problem that had occurred earlier in the year in the city jail.

To take care of the wounded in the war, a new hospital was being built in Richmond and was to be named in honor of Dr. Hunter Holmes McGuire, a Confederate surgeon who served with General Thomas J. "Stonewall" Jackson during the Civil War. The hospital was designed for 1,700 beds and would continue to be used after the war. To meet the needs of those wounded in combat, the hospital was rushed to completion.

Christmas shopping began in early November. No one could recall a time when shopping had started so early. However, there was a problem. There was a shortage of pennies. Because of this shortage, shoppers were asked to get out their piggy banks and "free the pennies" for circulation, including the steel pennies minted in 1943, to save copper. Copper was considered essential for the war effort. However, shoppers were glad to learn that copper pennies would be minted again in 1944 using discarded shell casings. People frequently confused steel pennies with dimes, and the pennies tended to rust in high-humidity areas like Richmond.

As Thanksgiving drew near, Christmas shopping had to stop for a few days while people prepared for Thanksgiving Day. The newspapers reported that there would be many union Thanksgiving services. There were also stories that there might be more turkeys available for Thanksgiving dinner, but Richmonders were warned that onion-flavored stuffing would be scarce. However, turkeys were not as plentiful as expected, and onions were almost unavailable, but the public still observed the day with prayers of thanksgiving "that victory is so much nearer this year than it was on Thanksgiving 1942."

Shopping for Christmas resumed after Thanksgiving. A reporter wrote, "Downtown stores were packed to the gills with Christmas shoppers and the weather did a typically Virginia dipsy-doo," but outside of Christmas and the weather, there was not much in the way of local news. As the shoppers paused to remember Pearl Harbor Day, an editorial in the *Richmond News Leader* posed this question, "Did those Japanese madmen think two years ago today that they would trap and destroy the whole of the American battle fleet at Pearl Harbor? Instead of an expansion, it began the extinction of their empire."

While remembering Pearl Harbor and shopping for Christmas, people became concerned about the large number of shoeshine boys on Broad Street and Hull Street. In response, the city confined all shoeshine boys "to specially designated spots north of Broad Street and west of Hull Street." Additionally, only two shoeshine boys could operate at any single corner, and they had to be in designated spaces painted on the sidewalk.

With the shoeshine boy situation resolved, the news again focused on Christmas. It was reported that 95 percent of Richmond's restaurants would be closed on Christmas Day, so a plea was made for citizens to invite servicemen to eat in their homes. To invite a serviceman to dinner, it was necessary to fill out a form printed in the paper and mail it to the USO, which would serve as a clearinghouse. Because Richmond was segregated, the forms had a block to check regarding race. Several thousand Richmond families responded to the request to have soldiers eat with them on Christmas.

The black market in rationed goods surfaced at Christmas. It was reported that some whiskey stores were selling nylons under the counter. The scheme was that a customer would whisper something about nylons, and a clerk would pull them from under the counter and, in a low voice, mention the price. When the money was paid, the sale was complete. Toys for children at Christmas consisted of train construction sets, navy construction sets, army construction sets, dart games, toy machine guns, kiddie cars and home bowling games. To add to the spirit of the holidays, it was also announced that some servicemen planned to ride around Richmond in a hay truck and sing Christmas carols.

Christmas in Richmond was quiet. Most businesses were closed, and more than five thousand soldiers were being entertained in private homes. Once again, there was no community Christmas pageant in Richmond. Midnight services were held in many churches along with Christmas Day services. In a Christmas editorial, the newspaper commented, "It may seem our undeserved affliction that this Christmas of 1943 should find our boys scattered around the world, in jungle and on mountain, in Arctic winter and on burning seas. These things are of the blackness of the night of travail. The star leads on. Have faith!" Yet the joy of Christmas was tempered by such phrases as "missing in action," "killed in action" and "wounded in action."

By the end of December, many men and women who had served their nation with honor were discharged from the service for various reasons, including injuries and the completion of their tours of duty. It was being reported that some of these former soldiers and sailors, who appeared to be in good health, were asked why they were not fighting the war. To avoid the embarrassment of providing an explanation to a nosy citizen, a special lapel pin was made available for them to wear. The pins displayed an eagle within a circle. Most soldiers referred to it as a "ruptured duck," but apparently the pin answered a lot of questions by letting the curious know that the wearer had served his country.

As the old year ended, an editorial writer observed that "1943 opened with the Germans at the gates of Stalingrad; and in the Pacific, the United States forces were just beginning to crack the Japanese forces in New Guinea." The writer continued, "Now, everywhere, though the darkest hours may lie immediately ahead, the slaves of the Nazis know that the bright days of their liberation will come." Then the old year passed away, and it was 1944.

# CHAPTER 6

# "OK, LET'S GO," 1944

*There will be a sad day coming for the foes of all mankind*
*They must answer to the people and it troubles their mind*
*Everybody who must fear them will rejoice on that great day*
*When the powers of dictators shall be taken all away.*

*There'll be smoke on the water, on the land and the sea*
*When our Army and Navy overtake the enemy.*
*There'll be smoke on the mountains where the heathen gods stay*
*And the sun that is shining will go down on that day.*
*—Earl Nunn and Zeke Clements*

The people in Richmond, Virginia, and the rest of the free world were growing tired of war. But 1944 began better than the previous year. The *Richmond Times-Dispatch* termed it the "Year of Decision." Most people had adjusted to rationing, frequent bond drives, Victory Gardens and efforts to collect junk, tin cans and fat. The one thing that no one could ever get used to, or really prepare for, was a dreaded telegram from the War Department stating in terse language that a loved one was dead, missing in action, wounded or taken prisoner. It is difficult to comprehend the stress under which this nation lived at a time when the world was in flames and anxiety gripped everyone. Adding to the stress was that people knew that Europe was going to be invaded, but they did not know when, where or how.. Each day was filled with anticipation, anxiety and uncertainty.

A Nazi armband removed from a dead German soldier by Ed Melton. *Judith Reynolds Johnson Collection.*

Many servicemen who knew Richmond women began sending them souvenirs from the battlefield. One woman received a propaganda leaflet like the ones being dropped on Japan. Another woman got a Japanese bracelet, a grass skirt and other trinkets from the South Seas. Marie Maddox Sarnoski received a different kind of gift. She was presented the Medal of Honor that was awarded to her husband, Second Lieutenant Joseph Sarnoski, who was a crew member on a B-17. Although gravely wounded, he kept firing a machine gun at enemy aircraft. He died before the plane landed, but his courage and sacrifice saved the crew, who would live to fight again. His twenty-three-year-old widow received America's highest award for valor in the presence of generals and colonels at the Richmond Air Base. Sarnoski's father could not attend the presentation because he had to mine coal in Pennsylvania so that other fathers' sons would be able to continue the fight for liberation.

When Richmond's servicemen came home from the war on furloughs, they were frequently interviewed, and their stories were published in the newspaper. Technical Sergeant Ashburn L. High, a waist gunner on a B-24 Liberator named Pistol Packin' Mama, had just completed the required twenty-five missions over Germany. The highly decorated gunner said in an interview that "war is a hellish mess." Then he commented, "You never know how good it is to live until you get back from a mission and feel the ground under you. Although German pilots are good, flak [anti-aircraft fire] is the real enemy of all flyers. There's nothing to do about it. You just have to take it; you cannot maneuver to evade it."

Less heroic was the fact that twenty sailors, eighteen soldiers and two marines were arrested in Richmond on various morals charges. Also arrested were ninety-two civilians for being "not of good fame in a moral sense," and fifty-eight more were arrested on charges of committing immoral acts. Prostitution was a crime that had the constant attention of the police, but they seemed powerless to stop it and the inevitable spread of venereal diseases. This plague was not discussed in polite company. Fortunately, Richmond had a VD hospital at 108 West Cary Street where men and women were treated for venereal diseases. In late spring, there were about one hundred men and women in the hospital. As an act of good will, the City of Richmond purchased six Bibles, eight dozen packs of playing cards and some jigsaw puzzles for them. A cynic commented that "there was more interest in playing games than reading Scripture." Also made available to the patients was penicillin, which was called the new miracle drug. The general treatment was to start with sulfa, and if that did not work, penicillin was used.

The Hotel Jefferson, the city's most famous and historic hotel, caught fire in March. The upper floors of the hotel were gutted by flames that swept through the east wing of the massive building and filled it with smoke. The newspaper reported that "the historic old hotel was a shambles. Most of the rooms were blackened with soot, doors bore the splintered marks of axes, and every room revealed the hasty flight of people." Truck Company Number 1 of the Richmond Fire Department arrived on the scene, but its eighty-five-foot extension ladder would not reach the sixth floor. A scaling ladder was then used to reach state delegate Edward De Jarnette of Ashland. Lost in the conflagration was Mrs. James Hubert Price, widow of the former governor of Virginia James Price, and state senator Aubrey G. Weaver, known as the "kingfish of legislative history." A total of six people died, and more than twenty people were injured in the fire.

Then there was a tragedy of a different kind. June Bug, the first plane to be named for a Richmond woman, was lost. Mrs. Sydney R. Jeter Jr. received two letters on the same day. One letter was from her husband, and she tore it open. It was his usual cheery letter. Then she opened the other letter. It was from the bombardier on her husband's plane. He told the young wife that her husband's plane had crashed over England following a bombing raid and that her husband and most of the crew of June Bug had been killed.

CONFIDENTIAL

WAR DEPARTMENT
A. A. F. Form No. 14
(Revised May 15, 1942)

ACCIDENT NO. _____

WAR DEPARTMENT
U. S. ARMY AIR FORCES
REPORT OF AIRCRAFT ACCIDENT

(1) Place 3½ mi. SW of Raunds, Northants (2) Date 22 February, 1944 (3) Time 0932

AIRCRAFT 4) Type and model B-17G (5) A. F. No. 42-38041 (6) Station AAF 107
Organization: (7) 8th AF (8) 303rd Bomb (9) 358th Bombardment
(Command and Air Force)    (Group)    (Squadron)

PERSONNEL

| Duty (10) | NAME (Last name first) (11) | RATING (12) | SERIAL No. (13) | RANK (14) | PERSONNEL CLASS (15) | BRANCH (16) | AIR FORCE OR COMMAND (17) | RESULT TO PERSONNEL (18) | USE OF PARACHUTE (19) |
|---|---|---|---|---|---|---|---|---|---|
| P | STUERMER, JOHN W. | P | O-802157 | 1st Lt. | 2C-1 | AC | 8th AF | Fatal | |
| CP | REYNOLDS, CHARLES L. | P | O-740922 | 2nd Lt. | 2C-1 | AC | 8th AF | Fatal | |
| N | TIEDMAN, WILLIAM A. | N | O-808193 | 2nd Lt. | 2C-1 | AC | 8th AF | Fatal | |
| B | NEWMAN, CLYDE D. | B | O-686120 | 2nd Lt. | 2C-1 | AC | 8th AF | Fatal | |
| E | HARRIS, DAVID B. | E | 35638585 | T/Sgt. | 2E-1 | AC | 8th AF | Fatal | |
| R | MURRAY, EDWARD F. | R | 11043735 | S/Sgt. | 2E-1 | AC | 8th AF | Fatal | |
| G | MILLER, DAVID I. | G | 11111894 | Sgt. | 2E-1 | AC | 8th AF | None | S |
| G | STARK, JOSEPH | G | 32460633 | S/Sgt. | 2E-1 | AC | 8th AF | Fatal | |
| G | COLLINS, MARVIN B. | G | 34506470 | S/Sgt. | 2E-1 | AC | 8th AF | Fatal | |
| G | CARROLL, MARVIN W. | G | 6333651 | Sgt. | 2E-1 | AC | 8th AF | Fatal | |

PILOT CHARGED WITH ACCIDENT

(20) STUERMER, JOHN W. (21) O-802157 (22) 1st Lt. (23) 2C-1 (24) AC
(Last name first)    (Middle initial)    (Serial number)    (Rank)    (Personnel Class)    (Branch)

Assigned (25) 8th AF (26) 303rd Bomb (27) 358th Bombardment (28) AAF 107
(Command and Air Force)    (Group)    (Squadron)    (Station)

Attached for flying (29) 8th AF (30) 303rd Bomb (31) 358th Bombardment (32) AAF 107
(Command and Air Force)    (Group)    (Squadron)    (Station)

Original rating (33) Pilot (34) Apr. 20, 43 Present rating (35) Pilot (36) Apr. 20, 43 Instrument rating (37) Aug. 30, 1943
(Rating)    (Date)    (Rating)    (Date)    (Date)

FIRST PILOT HOURS:
(at the time of this accident)
(38) This type 283:35  (42) Instrument time last 6 months 5:00
(39) This model 79:55  (43) Instrument time last 30 days 1:00
(40) Last 90 days 124:45  (44) Night time last 6 months 50:40
(41) Total 391:45  (45) Night time last 30 days 2:00

AIRCRAFT DAMAGE

DAMAGE    (49) LIST OF DAMAGED PARTS
(46) Aircraft  W  W  W  W    Complete Wreck - 12X500 LB Bombs in Aircraft.
(47) Engines  W  W  W  W    Exploded in Wreck.
(48) Propeller  W  W  W  W

(50) Weather at the time of accident Visibility 1,800 YDS with snow, Ceiling 2,500 feet, with top of 6,000 feet. Clouds 7/10 to 8/10.

(51) Was the pilot flying on instruments at the time of accident
(52) Cleared from AAF 107 (53) To AAF 107 (54) Kind of clearance Contact

(55) Pilot's mission Combat Mission

(56) Nature of accident Mid Air Collision

(57) Cause of accident Gp. Leader flew formation too close

June Bug accident report showing the death of most of its crew. *United States Air Force.*

The young wife had become a widow, and a gold star replaced the blue one in the window of her home on Victor Street.

On March 25, 1944, Jack Kilpatrick commented on what had changed in Richmond since the start of the war. He wrote:

*A few things are different. The shop windows feature a lot of uniforms for sale and a couple of penny arcades have sprung up on the north side of Broad Street. Grace and Franklin Streets are crowded with visiting soldiers and sailors until the small hours of the morning and the shoeshine boys are reaping a harvest. The newspaper salesmen still trot up and down shouting pee-po* [paper], *and sunny days see the familiar flower stalls in operation near the Sixth Street Market.*

He further reported:

*The number of women trolley and bus operators has increased; and all of the restaurants are closed one day a week; hotels are packed; and lines a block long are curling away from theater arcades. The skyline hasn't changed a square brick; the girls are just as pretty, the churches just as crowded. It's the same old city on the James...*

Richmonders in the military must have found some comfort in the fact that their hometown was at least one thing that had not changed in their lives.

March went out like a lion with a severe sleet storm, but it did not stop those planning their Victory Gardens. Children were flying paper kites in the parks, and roller skates with their metal wheels could be heard throughout the neighborhoods. The sounds of fire engines coming out of the station on Forest Hill Avenue could again be heard. For many months, the station had been closed because of the lack of firefighters, and it was now able to reopen with auxiliary firemen. Also heard was the German language spoken by the prisoners of war who were working in a Richmond lumberyard.

Easter 1944 was celebrated in Richmond with church services and the traditional parade. There was a sunrise service on the steps of the Virginia State Capitol under the sponsorship of the Federation of Christian Young People. The Easter Parade had many servicemen and servicewomen walking along with Richmonders whose fashion consciousness had been modified by the rather plain attire demanded by wartime dress regulations. In evidence also were many baby carriages pushed by mothers whose husbands were fighting a war so that Richmonders could always have an Easter Parade.

Unlike past Easters, eggs were plentiful, and Easter egg hunts were again possible, but there were no chocolate bunnies. Richmonders were also reminded that Easter was being celebrated on the battlefields. The Associated Press reported, "It was an Easter without the trimmings, held in rain and mud in some sectors, and under a canopy of whistling shells in others. In fashion were the steel helmets of war with guns in readiness, tanks fully fueled, howitzers with set trajectories, and foxholes and other shelters of safety within a short distance."

One of the most emotional events in Richmond was Mothers' Day. People wore red carnations if their mothers were alive and white ones if they had died. But the real focus in 1944 was on all of the mothers who had sons or daughters in service. The *Richmond News Leader* carried an emotional article by Jack Kilpatrick, who wrote, "The war had produced heroes by the score, citations, medals, tales of bravery—these are gluts on a market based on valor. Yet, no battle has yet produced a symbol of courage stronger than the women whose lives are bound up in the stars in the windows."

Even during the war, some people did really weird things. On one occasion, a woman decided to play a prank on a neighbor, and she ordered seven hearses to be sent to her neighbor's house in the 2600 block of East Marshall Street. It was a cruel hoax that did not seem to evoke much humor from anyone, especially the funeral home and the police department. Another tale that made the rounds was about a Richmond woman who had divorced fourteen husbands and was not getting along with number fifteen. Eventually, she filed suit for a divorce from her fifteenth husband "alleging that he taunted her about her first fourteen marriages and hit her with his artificial leg."

On a positive note, the Department of Public Works was authorized to employ twenty-six African American men to solve the street-cleaning problem. In the past, only white men held these jobs. Although this was hailed as a step in the right direction, seventy-five out of seventy-nine white men in the bureau threatened to go on strike if blacks were hired. Eventually, the force was integrated, with a special building in Jackson Ward provided for the black workers who were being supervised by black managers. These men were the first of their race to have these jobs, and the threat of a strike ended.

It was also announced that the Aircraft Warning Service, including Civilian Filter Center operators and the Ground Observer Corps, would cease

Airplane spotter cards used by members of the Aircraft Warning System. *Author's collection.*

operation, but air-raid tests would continue. One of the Aircraft Warning volunteers was Ruby Decker, who stood watch on a platform at Hotchkiss Field in the North Side of Richmond scanning the skies for enemy aircraft. Like all airplane spotters, she used a deck of cards with pictures of airplanes on them to tell the difference between a Flying Fortress and a Heinkel-111. In a letter given to her by the secretary of war, she was thanked for her service to the nation. She was also advised that "you have learned many facts which, if made public, might be of service to the enemy…The obligation you assumed to safeguard military information remains in full effect." The end of the Aircraft Warning Service suggested that if an airplane were seen in the sky, it would be friendly.

Although the threat of an attack on United States soil seemed unlikely, an attack on Fortress Europe was eminent. The waiting ended when General Eisenhower sent a message to the troops who were preparing to invade Fortress Europe and attack Field Marshall Erwin Rommel's Atlantic Wall. The general wrote:

> *Soldiers, Sailors, and Airmen of the Allied Expeditionary Force. You are about to embark upon the Great Crusade toward which we have striven these many months. The eyes of the world are upon you. The hopes and prayers of liberty-loving people everywhere march with you.*

And then it happened! General Eisenhower said, "OK, let's go," and these words launched the greatest invasion in human history. From the Supreme Headquarters of the Allied Expeditionary Force, the invasion known as Operation Overlord was announced to a waiting world at 7:32 a.m. Greenwich Mean Time (3:32 a.m. Eastern War Time in Richmond). People heard about it in various ways. The news first came at 5:00 a.m. in Richmond when the bells of St. James's Episcopal Church broke the silence of dawn. For many Richmonders, this is how they learned the invasion was taking place. Others learned from the newspaper, the radio or neighbor calling neighbor. The *Richmond Times-Dispatch* ran this headline, "Allies Storming Inland in France: Beachhead Quickly Gained." The headline in an extra edition had only one word in large, bold type: "INVASION." D-day had arrived! Most Richmonders were relieved that the invasion had begun and that the agonizing days of waiting were over.

Military leaders were generally optimistic about the invasion, but everyone dreaded the casualty lists, which would soon be published. The *Richmond News Leader* reported, "Losses so far were small and the opposition by the Nazis was unexpectedly slight." (This would prove to be overly optimistic, especially for the Richmonders in the Twenty-ninth Division.) The *Richmond News Leader* stated that "this 6th of June will be forever memorable in the history of Europe." In retrospect, it was one of the most important days in world history.

News of the invasion was everywhere. Radios broadcasted only invasion news, movies showed newsreels of the invasion and the newspapers were filled with information from the Normandy beaches. Many businesses closed, and Miller and Rhoads covered all of its windows with gold curtains

Newspaper announcing the invasion of Europe. *Author's collection.*

and placed lighted candles and written prayers in them. The Free World held its collective breath while the Allied forces forged ahead, but the cost was terrific.

Generally, war correspondents did not write about the human carnage in the newspapers, but the human wreckage from the invasion was beyond comprehension. Field hospitals were filled with dying men with limbs blown away and faces mutilated beyond recognition. Men screamed for their mothers as they took their last breaths. To see the mutilated bodies could drive a person insane. Maybe the lucky ones were those who died on the beach and never knew the pain and agony of a horrible death in a field hospital. And there were many dead soldiers strewn across the sands of Normandy. As soldiers were dying, Richmonders prayed and prayed.

At Highland Park Elementary School, sixth-grader Betty Hach stood in the auditorium and offered this prayer for her school:

> *We are gathered here in the auditorium because we know now that the invasion has started. We pray that the terrible war will be over. Dear Lord,*

A Sherman tank used by the Allied forces during the war. *Photograph by Walter Griggs.*

*please be with all the boys, especially those hurt and dying. We pray that there will never be any more wars. Lord, we ask that you teach us the way that we will always have peace.*

She then asked that everyone join her in the Lord's Prayer.

Speaking from Washington, President Roosevelt led Americans in a prayer that opened with these words: "Almighty God, Our sons, the pride of our nation, this day have set upon a mighty endeavor, a struggle to preserve our republic, our religion, and our civilization and set free a suffering humanity..." The people of Richmond flocked to houses of worship that were kept open for prayer. Clergymen visited courts, industrial centers and businesses to offer prayers for the success of the invasion. Most churches and synagogues had an 8:00 p.m. evening service, and services were also held in the schools. Only church bells broke the silence of D-Day. Richmond had ruled against sirens or anything that appeared festive since many men would surely die as they waded ashore on the beaches of Normandy.

The newspapers were filled with ads from local businesses in support of the invasion. Jurgens Furniture Company published the following:

> *Yes, our boys are on the march—fighting, suffering, and dying—that we may live. There may be a few hide-bound wretches among us whose hearts do not bleed for them, but most of us would gladly give his all if thereby the burdens of our boys could be made easier and an early peace assured.*

Bullington's Paint and Wallpaper published this thought, "Our faith in ourselves and in the future is involved with our daily efforts to maintain the freedom for which we are fighting." Thalhimers proclaimed, "Lafayette, we are here!" Byramn's Restaurant suggested, "Like well-trained tigers they have patiently awaited the most opportune moment to strike—the fighting forces of America and her allies have sprung upon the oppressors of right and justice in a final desperate fight for Victory…that victory must be ours!" Walter D. Moses, a music store, affirmed, "It is the solemn duty of every man and woman, boy and girl to go to church today and pray for Divine guidance for our men—and the leaders of our men." Kaufman's simply stated, "A prayer for a speedy Victory, and abiding peace!"

While men were dying on the beaches of Normandy, there was an article in the newspaper about "Jealous Wives" who doubted the faithfulness of their husbands while they were away. Dorothy Dix commented:

> *Considering that every wife represents her husband's taste in women and that he picked her out from all the balance of her sex because she was his heart's desire, it would seem that wives should be immune to jealousy. For all women know that while they have to take what they can get in marriage, men can take their choice, and so when one gives up his bachelor freedom and undertakes the support of a woman, it is because he wants her above everything else in the world.*

Women should certainly have felt better after reading this!

Some of the concerned women might have had spouses who bombed Japan with the new B-29 Super Fortresses for the first time on June 15. The story of the bombing was terse: "B-29 Super Fortresses of the United States Army Air Forces Twentieth Bomber Command bombed Japan today." This was the first attack on the Japanese mainland since the Doolittle Raid in April 1942. These planes would make many more bomb runs over Japan and would eventually drop the bomb that would end World War II.

Newly completed McGuire Hospital began to receive patients, and to enable them to make three-minute long-distance phone calls home, the newspaper started a "Telephone Subscription Fund." Soldiers were arriving directly from combat areas, and their greatest wish was to make phone calls to loved ones. Many companies and individuals sent checks, including the Chesapeake and Ohio Railway, Friedman-Marks Clothing Store, the staff of McGuire's Hospital, Chimborazo School and "Six-Girls with Someone in the Service." Boys and girls in Ginter Park and Barton Heights went door-to-door trying to fill a half-gallon Mason jar with money. Joining them was a group called the Floyd Avenue Wildcats and the Junior War Workers. One eleven-year-old girl raised over $100 for the fund. In appreciation, she was given an insignia from the uniform of a German paratrooper.

Another War Bond Drive opened with a parade down Grace Street featuring tanks, cavalry, sailors, soldiers, marines, engineers and mechanized equipment. An additional attraction was a barrage balloon that could be seen floating over Capitol Square. These balloons were used in Europe and other places to destroy low-flying planes trying to attack a city. Steel cables held them in place, and attached to the cables were explosives. If a low-flying airplane happened to hit one of the cables, it would fly no more. An officer with the balloon said, "The psychological effect of a mass of balloons upon enemy pilots is one of the outstanding assets, since the balloons are staggered so that a plane cannot fly through them without coming into contact with the wires." If a Richmonder looked into the air over Capitol Square, he would remember that War Bond Drive. Also, by looking at Capitol Square, you could see a large billboard that obscured the bell tower. The poster showed an American flag with the slogan: "Buy US Defense and War Bonds Now." There were some objections to both displays, but they remained.

Then the dreaded casualty reports from Normandy began to be published. Ensign Winfield Nelms Kyle Jr. was killed in action during the Normandy Invasion. He was the first Richmonder to be reported as killed in the invasion. A graduate of the University of Richmond, he received his commission at Northwestern University. He was killed when the landing craft he commanded was hit by German artillery. Many more names would be added to the list of those who died at Normandy—those who had the courage to charge into firing German machine guns. Where did this nation get men with such courage? One chaplain wrote that "courage is fear that has said its prayers."

On July 4, the first mail reached Richmond from one of the soldiers who had landed at Normandy. The letter was from a member of the Twenty-ninth Division, which had many Richmonders in its ranks. The soldier wrote, "Tell a friend that a little Virginia regiment cracked that wall on the French coast, and those boys died like Virginians." The letter was longer, but it was not published with the notation that you probably could not read it "through your tears."

Shortly after the invasion, the newspapers began to carry many notices of Richmonders who had died in combat. One man who was killed was Lieutenant J.W. Montieth Jr., who died on the Normandy Beach. But he did more than charge across a French beach. A graduate of Thomas Jefferson High School, he was drafted into the army in October 1941. The Citation for the Medal of Honor received by his mother stated that he "led tanks on foot through a minefield and into firing position. Under his leadership, his men captured an advantageous position. He continued to ignore his own personal safely, repeatedly crossing the 200 to 300 yards of open terrain under heavy fire. He was eventually killed by enemy fire."

The newspapers had many ways of listing casualties, including the following: "Four men with kin here give their lives in service," "Two Richmonders die in action," "Two Richmond soldiers give lives in battle," "Richmonder killed, two are prisoners, another missing," "Two Richmonders, among six Virginians, giving lives in service," "One Richmonder gives life, one in Nazi War Prison, and eight are wounded," "Sergeant Green gives life in France" and "Two here previously reported missing now reported killed."

There were also frequent reports about Richmonders in combat. Lieutenant John W. Boucher was in command of a landing ship when he picked up some seagoing hitchhikers, including General Dwight D. Eisenhower, Admiral Harold R. Starke, General Omar Bradley, Air Marshall Arthur Tedder of the Royal Air Force and Eisenhower's aid, Major General John C.H. Lee. As they approached Normandy, there was a large explosion on the beach that shook the ship and caused soot from the smokestack to get all over the officers. Lieutenant Boucher commented, "I was embarrassed to death, but after they left I had a good laugh about it."

Brave men were dying in the war, but some individuals apparently did not have a sense of patriotism and fell victim to avoid-the-war scams. In one scam, a man paid fifty dollars for a "hoodoo pill," which was supposed to make a person so sick that he would have to be discharged from the service. It did not work. In a similar scam, two men were fined fifty dollars for selling a man a method to avoid the draft. The recipe was to put "a kerosene-soaked rag around the abdomen for several days to cause a stomach ailment." It did not work, either. In a more serious criminal matter, the FBI arrested Waldemar Othmer, a naturalized American citizen and a former resident of Richmond, on a charge of conspiracy to violate the espionage statutes. It was revealed that he was trained in Germany as an espionage agent and had recently tried to purchase material that was used to make secret ink.

In other local news, it was reported that Miss Wow, a black Belgian shepherd dog, was awarded two gold stars because two of her offspring, Ghillie and Ghent, were killed in the service of their country. On a less patriotic note, "three fire engines responded to a call from a fire alarm box when a lady tried to put a letter in the box at First and Franklin Streets." For obvious reasons, the firemen were not happy. But apparently, the three ladies avoided a trip in the Black Maria (truck used to transport prisoners to jail). And there was one additional problem. Women were causing a ruckus when they bought shoes. A shoe store employee commented that there was a "time when womanhood was modest and even the edge of a toenail or the pink of a heel showing through her stocking was utterly horrible and so terribly embarrassing to milady." But the salesman said, "Today, women come in with bare feet or with bare legs and feet covered with flimsy little foot-lets and expect to get a good fit in a pair of shoes which is next to impossible." It seemed that moral decadence had struck the shoe stores.

Amid the horrors of war, a cruel disease began to strike Richmond's children and the children of the nation. It was called infantile paralysis, or polio, and cases were sweeping Virginia. Parents did not know how to protect their children from this disease and its paralyzing effect. In some places, church services were not held and schools were closed. In Richmond, physicians were instructing parents to keep their children away from theaters, schools and other public gatherings. Although there was pressure to keep the schools closed, they did open, but many parents kept their children home as advised by their physicians. The polio epidemic added to the stress of mothers who had husbands in combat zones and children who could catch and be permanently crippled, or die, from this mysterious disease.

Meanwhile, wounded soldiers from the Normandy invasion were arriving at McGuire's Hospital and were making free phone calls to their loved ones. One veteran said to a Red Cross worker after making a free call, "I am so happy I could kiss you." Other comments included, "I just called home and found out I am the father of a baby girl," "I talked to my two-year-old daughter who had not been born when I went overseas," "My wife and I could not think of what to say to each other." One father heard for the first time, "Hello, Daddy," when he talked to the son whom he had never seen. In addition to free phone calls, Richmonders embraced the wounded heroes by providing books, trips to the circus, furniture and many other things they needed.

Vesper Services were held at the Carillon on Sundays at 5:00 p.m. during the war years. On one Sunday, the Revered Arthur W. Newell of St. John's Evangelical Lutheran Church conducted the service. Unfortunately, the Word of the Lord was drowned out by a low-flying airplane that was circling the Carillon during the service. One irate citizen wrote, "There certainly must be some way to keep these men from flying around the Carillon during the one hour in which vespers are being conducted. It is one thing for a minister to compete with quacking ducks, honking geese, and chatting squirrels, but it is not easy to compete with a noisy yellow plane during the service." Reverend Newell continued to preach to those in attendance.

Mayor Gordon Ambler, who had served as Richmond's mayor since the beginning of the war, was succeeded by William C. Herbert on September 1, 1944. The media lauded the accomplishments of the outgoing mayor and viewed this as a smooth transition. According to tradition, the new mayor had to bring his own furniture for his office.

On September 8, 1944, it was announced that another Richmonder was to be honored by having a ship named after him. Ensign Horace A. Bass Jr., the first Richmond Professional Institute graduate to die in the war, was to be so honored. Assigned to the USS *Yorktown*, he died a hero in the Battle of Midway by shooting down a Japanese dive-bomber and fighter even though his plane was severely damaged. The USS *Bass* was a high-speed transport and was christened by his young widow at the Bethlehem Steel Company at Fore River in Quincy, Massachusetts.

Although the war was raging on two fronts, there was a slow dismantling of the war installations that had moved to Richmond after Pearl Harbor. In early October, it was announced that the antiaircraft unit at the Mosque would relocate to Fort Bliss, Texas; the Patent Office would move back to Washington as soon as space became available; and the *Merrimac*, which had been located at Broad and Sixth Streets, was going to be moved. The model of the Confederate ironclad was a wartime landmark. It was not only a navy recruiting station but also had been the site for patriotic programs and War Bond rallies, a meeting place for servicemen from all over the United States and the venue of other events. Because of a shortage of naval personnel to man the station, it was donated to the Boy Scouts of America and moved to Lakeside. And to the relief of everyone, there would be no more blackouts.

Richmonders, in many small ways, started looking to a time when the war would end. For example, Harris-Flippen Sporting Goods Store had a supply of shotgun shells that sold at a record rate, and Thalhimers had a sportsmen show with live animals. Unfortunately, the black bear got loose but was caught by a shopper who was slightly injured but did not get a Purple Heart. The state Chamber of Commerce began making plans for the postwar tourist trade, and a history commission was established to preserve the history of the conflict. If nothing else, these events showed that the end of the war might be in sight and that the city could return to normal.

Many Richmonders, however, were still in combat, and their stories continued to be published in the newspapers. In one case, Second Lieutenant Marion L. Woolard, a P51 Mustang pilot from Richmond, destroyed a German Messerschmitt 109 in aerial combat. The lieutenant wrote of his victory as follows, "About twenty-five Jerries jumped the bomber we were escorting to Merseburg. I went after one of them and followed it down through the clouds. I fired at it and saw hits along its fuselage and wings. I closed to within about fifty feet, right behind it and cut loose. The German plane crashed going about 250 miles per hour. The pilot did not get out."

In another story, Second Lieutenant Clarence F. Wasser of Richmond was the navigator on a B-24 Liberator bomber assigned to the Seventh Air Force. After dropping bombs on Iwo Jima, the plane was hit in the nose compartment, the top turret, the hydraulic lines, the throttle controls and two of the four engines; oil was leaking out from the plane along with gas; and there was a gaping hole in the rudder. With the pilot and copilot wounded, a gunner who had washed out of pilot training brought the plane in safely and saved the crew. The plane split in two upon landing. The B-24, known as either House of Bourbon or Chambermaid, had made its last flight, but its crew was safe. Truly, it had come in on a "wing and a prayer."

By reading the newspapers, Richmonders got used to the various datelines that told the global expanse of the war. Datelines included the

Postcard showing a B-24 Liberator bomber. *Author's collection.*

following: "Supreme Headquarters Allied Expeditionary Force, Pearl Harbor, Honolulu"; "With United States Parachute Troops"; "A B-26 Base Somewhere in England"; "Aboard the USS *Santa Fe* in the Western Pacific"; and "Aboard the USS *Richmond* in the Pacific," to mention only a few. The Richmond newspapers carried a wide range of comic strips that relieved some people from the daily stress of war. Popular comic strips included: *Blondie, Mickey Finn, Barnaby, Li'l Abner, Moon Mullins, Jane Arden, Henry, The Gumps, Big Chief Wahoo, Terry and the Pirates, Joe Palooka, Orphan Annie* and *Superman*. Although many comics had military themes, *Superman* did not enlist because he failed the eye test. His X-ray vision pierced the first eye chart, and he read the chart in another room.

The radio also provided a diversion for avid listeners of soap operas, including the following: *A Date with Judy, Guiding Light, Ma Perkins, Right to Happiness, Backstage Wife, Stella Dalles, Lorenzo Jones, A Girl Marries* and *Portia Faces Life*. I can remember some of these because I listened to them when I was sick. I can recall one story line where an inventor put a device in a car that would say, "Going too fast" if the speed limit was exceeded. Unfortunately, the inventor did not tell the driver about the new device, and when the driver was admonished about excessive speed, she crashed the car. I cannot recall the nature of her injuries.

Shows and movies were also popular. Richmond had a large number of movie theaters, including the Carillon, Capitol, Grand, Colonial, State, Westhampton, Bellevue, Brookland, Venus, Ponton and Lowes. Some of the popular movies included the following: *God Is My Co-Pilot*, *The Rats of Tobruk*, *Navy Comes Through*, *The Fighting Seebeas*, *So Proudly We Hail*, *Bomber's Moon*, *They Were Expendable* and *The Cross of Lorraine*.

Halloween provided some forms of entertainment. After several orderly celebrations, this one got out of control. On Halloween night, fifteen thousand Richmond youngsters took part in the festivities at the various playgrounds, and there were twenty-seven calls to the police to restore order. Some of the calls were as follows: disorderly boys in rear of convent; disorderly boys in playground; disorderly boys on Grove Avenue; boys burning leaves; boys putting soap on streetcar tracks; someone throwing rocks at streetlights; boys stopping a streetcar; and many, many more. Apparently, Richmond girls behaved themselves, with possibly one exception. One young lady sent her boyfriend a personally recorded phonograph record to play. The contents remain unknown, but it is known that the soldier inadvertently played it over a loudspeaker in five barracks, and the words of love were heard by hundreds of soldiers who enjoyed the chirping of a Richmond lovebird. This was probably more of a treat than a trick.

When Thanksgiving Day approached, there was a controversy over which day was really Thanksgiving Day. Presidents since Abraham Lincoln had always declared it to be the last Thursday in November. However, in 1944, President Roosevelt signed a bill declaring Thanksgiving Day to be the fourth Thursday of November. Since 1944 had five Thursdays, some states followed tradition and celebrated Thanksgiving on the last, or fifth, Thursday, and some followed the new federal law and celebrated it on the fourth Thursday. Governor Darden of Virginia declared Thanksgiving to be the last Thursday, but federal employees and all military installations in Virginia celebrated it on the fourth Thursday. So Virginia had two Thanksgiving Days, and some people celebrated both of them.

If two Thanksgiving Days were not complicated enough, an additional issue in Richmond concerned how men should behave around women. According to some women, chivalry was dead by 1944. Men no longer were offering seats on crowded buses to woman or doing other acts like letting women go through open doors first or getting off elevators first. One naval officer in Richmond commented upon his return from the Pacific Theater, "The girls don't give me a chance to whistle; they whistle first." Another

A German Lugar pistol used by the German army. *Author's collection.*

soldier suggested that "women like to be independent until they get in a tight spot. Then femininity is all over the place." It was also noted that "in Richmond nightspots, girls keep up with their male escorts drink by drink and out smoke them." The general explanation was that women had learned to look out for themselves and had learned to get along without men. Unfortunately, both men and women were drinking Solox, a shellac solvent, and fifteen had died from it. If Solox was not available, there was "Torpedo Juice." This lethal concoction was made by pouring antifreeze through a loaf of bread. (Do not try this. Present-day antifreeze is not the same as the antifreeze used in Torpedo Juice.) Another drink was called Moose Milk, but it was not popular in Richmond. However, Canadians seemed to have enjoyed it.

On a healthier note, Christmas shopping was in full swing, and children were writing to Santa. Boys were asking for toy soldiers, tinker toys, bows and arrows, horns, wooden guns and drums. Girls tended to ask for dolls, pots and pans and dollhouses made out of cardboard. One little boy showed the true Christmas spirit when he wrote, "Santa, please bring my little sister a doll." Most children did not know it, but their toys were made of wood, pasteboard and plastic and were not of prewar quality.

The Christmas season, however, was filled with fear and uncertainty. The Allies were making good progress in their movement across Europe when the picture suddenly changed. On December 16, 1944, Germany launched what would be its last great offensive: a desperate attack on the surging Allied armies at their weakest point. Led by Panzer tanks grinding through snow and followed by 250,000 of the German armies' best soldiers enduring bitter cold, Hitler's forces pushed a bulge seventy miles wide and fifty miles deep into the Allied lines. When the Germans demanded the surrender of the town of Bastogne, Brigadier General Anthony McAuliffe sent a one-word response to the German commander: "Nuts." General George Patton said in his unique way, "I'll go through the Germans like c--p through a goose." But General Patton was frustrated that the weather was bad and he could not get air support. In typical Patton fashion, he ordered Colonel James H. O'Neil, the Catholic chaplain, to write a prayer for clear weather. The chaplain wrote, "Almighty and merciful Father, we humbly beseech Thee, of thy great goodness, to restrain these immoderate rains with which we have had to contend…" The weather cleared, and the battle continued to rage for the rest of the year with mounting casualties. Many Americans were shot after they had surrendered at a place called Malmady. Once the Americans learned prisoners were being shot, the hell of war reached a new level of depravity—if such a thing was possible.

With a battle raging in Europe, Christmas was not merry. Most Richmonders spent time in their homes and in church. Churches were filled, and the worshippers were solemn. Turkey was not on many tables, nor was chicken, which was also hard to get. But the real difference from prewar Christmases were all of the empty chairs in Richmond homes, some of which would never be filled by their former occupants. An editorial in the Richmond newspaper commented, "Do not be one of those weaklings who draped the Christmas tree in crepe. It is not for you, descendants and friends of fighting men, to whine 'This is a black Christmas.' Instead, we should thank God and take courage."

In Richmond, New Year's Eve was quiet. There were some dances and parties, but people could not get the Battle of the Bulge off of their minds even though the tide was beginning to turn in favor of the Allies.

And far away from its namesake city, the USS *Richmond* was steaming in the icy north Pacific. Thousands of stars were twinkling in the brilliant midnight sky as it continued its lonely patrol. Only the sounds of the ship's

The USS *Richmond*, a cruiser, served in World War II. *National Archives.*

engine and the parting seas could be heard. Then the silence was broken when, following navy tradition, the ship's bell was rung eight times for the old year and eight times for the New Year. The bells let everyone on board know, whether they were on the bridge or sleeping in a hammock, that a new year had arrived.

No one knew it at the time, but by the next New Year's Eve, the USS *Richmond* would be headed for the scrap yard, and in its namesake city, the soldiers and sailors would be coming home.

# CHAPTER 7

# PEACE, 1945

*Let us pray that peace will be restored to the world and that God will preserve it always.*
*—General Douglas MacArthur, 1945*

*When the lights go on again all over the World*
*And the boys are home again all over the world*
*And rain or snow is all that may fall from the skies above*
*A kiss won't mean "goodbye" but "Hello to love."*

*When the lights go on again all over the world*
*And the ships will sail again all over the world*
*Then we'll have time for things like wedding rings and free hearts will sing*
*When the light go on again all over the world.*
*—Eddie Seller, Sol Marcus and Bennie Benjamin*

The first morning of the New Year opened with a brilliant rainbow in the western sky. Many people saw this as the foretelling of a better year in 1945. And the world needed a better year. The war had dragged on, and many Richmonders had been killed, wounded or were prisoners of war. Was 1945 going to be the year when the war would end and "lights would go on again all over the world"? Only time would tell, but in the meantime, life would go on with the fear and dread of what the next day might bring.

With a shortage of physicians, many Richmonders were depending on over-the-counter medications for their ills, and there were many remedies advertised in the newspapers. There was something for almost every ailment, including the following: P.D.S. Discovery killed bedbugs; Siticide killed scabies; Resinol helped sore feet; Juniper-Tar Compound was for chest colds; F and F was for sore throats; Bis-O-Carb was good for something or other, as was Nature's Remedy. Other products included Ben Gay, Mentholatum, Freezone and Espotabs. Of special interest to worn-out Richmonders might have been Scott's Emulsion, which was described as an excellent "tonic when you're feeling tired and rundown."

Music can also help you when you feel exhausted, which is why Richmonders were excited when an old friend returned to town. Eddie Weaver was remembered as the organist at the Lowe's Theater prior to the war. People were glad that he had been assigned to McGuire's Hospital to lead a band to entertain the sick and wounded. Also back home were Mickey and Donna, two pet ducks that had escaped from their coop. The police found the two ducks hiding, cold and wet, under a porch. The newspaper reported that the ducks refused to be photographed by the police. In the midst of war, Richmond had not lost its love of music, and police officers could still look for ducks.

The war caused families to separate, and this frequently caused problems in the form of flirting with married men. A single woman was interested in a married man with four children who was living a long way from his family. She had gone out with him several times and wondered if this might be a problem since she saw no harm in it and would avoid falling in love. Dorothy Dix, in a newspaper column, advised:

*You say that you know enough not to let yourself fall in love. Alas, my child, that is something that the wisest and strongest cannot say they will do or they will not do. There is an old adage about the danger of playing with fire that I would call to the attention of every girl who is tempted to have a flirtation with a fascinating, married man.*

Presumably this ended the flirtation, but I cannot be sure.

Problems in relationships were not the only issues. As more and more men entered the military, critical machines in war plants were left idle since there was no one to operate them. A reporter wrote, "Projectiles, ready for delivery, are stacked up in gleaming rows because laborers are not available to handle them." Many of these boxes had "Kilroy was here" scratched on them. This slogan was seen everywhere, but its origin remained a mystery.

A tank destroyer ad. *Author's collection.*

There were many pleas for men and women to seek employment in factories making critical items for the war effort. One song about women in the factories had this line: "She's the girl that makes the thing that drills the hole that holds the spring that drives the rod that turns the knob that works the thing-ummy-bob."

There were also pleas to plant more Victory Gardens, no matter how small the plot, since farmers could not meet the needs of all of the people at home and the servicemen abroad. Richmond also needed a second airport, but it seemed that no one wanted an airport near his home. It was reported that the latest reason not to build an airport at a particular location was that "the noise of the planes would damage the contentedness of the cows grazing below and, thereby, cause inferior milk and endanger the health of Richmond's children."

On the battlefront in January, the city learned that the United States Army had closed the bulge and was advancing toward Germany, and in February, the German Siegfried Line had been penetrated. It was also in February that the United States Marines landed on the island of Iwo Jima in the Pacific. This invasion and the bitterness of the fighting resulted in the comment that "uncommon valor was a common virtue." And then there was the news that made everyone proud.

Ernest Herbert Dervishian, a Richmond lawyer, received a battlefield commission as a second lieutenant and was awarded the Medal of Honor for capturing forty German soldiers and knocking out their machine guns while they were fighting in Italy. Upon his return to Richmond, Lieutenant Dervishian commented, "God's hand had been on my shoulder...I was lucky." He also felt that the knowledge of the German language that he had learned at John Marshall High School had helped him when he told the Germans in their own language to "come here with hands high—make haste." And Richmond saluted him with a parade, a plaque from the Richmond Bar Association, a life membership in the Chamber of Commerce and other honors. He was described by a reporter as "a whale of a nice guy."

Modesty seems to be a characteristic of American heroes. Joseph Becker enlisted in the U.S. Army early in 1941 and was a member of the 111th Field Artillery, which was part of the 29th Division that invaded Normandy. A master sergeant, he was in the thick of combat and probably served as a forward artillery observer. Remarkably, he survived the slaughter on Normandy Beach and was awarded the Bronze Star. The citation read, in part: "The high standards of courage, devotion to duty and discipline required during long periods of combat were met by Master Sergeant Becker in a manner that reflects great credit upon him and the military service..." However, this American soldier made no claim to being a hero. In a letter to his family, he wrote, "Although this is the same medal [bronze star] given for heroism in action, I did not get it for that reason, so please do not confuse it with a medal for heroic achievement. I make no claim to being a hero. It's simply this, the boss was pleased with my work and wanted to show his appreciation so he gave me a medal." This modest soldier did not want to be called a hero, but he was a hero who helped to liberate an enslaved people. By the end of the war, he had also earned the Good Conduct Medal, the American Defense Service Medal and the European African Middle Eastern Theater Service Medal. Like Lieutenant Dervishian, he was a modest man.

Although the war was still being fought, veterans who had completed their tours of duty were returning to Richmond and resuming their lives. Thirteen discharged veterans enrolled at the University of Richmond, while others enrolled at the Richmond Professional Institute under the GI Bill of Rights. Another hopeful sign of battlefield success was that all air-raid sirens were disconnected in Richmond to save electricity, and blackout curtains were

*Above*: The World War II
Memorial in Monroe Park.
*Photograph by Cara F. Griggs.*

*Left*: The raising of the United
States flag on Iwo Jima. *National
Archives.*

being removed from buildings, as was the black paint on the skylights. These
measures were no longer needed. The war had passed them by.

But the war had not ended, and people gathered in the Mosque to
dedicate a memorial to those Richmonders who had made the supreme
sacrifice in the war. The memorial was designed by Charles Gillette, a well-
known Richmond landscape architect, and was located in Monroe Park at
the corner of Franklin and Laurel Streets. It was a brick wall with plaques

of Tennessee marble on which would be inscribed the names of those Richmonders who were killed in the war. The service of dedication was held at the Mosque, with Christian and Jewish religious leaders participating. The Reverend E.E. Smith of Ebenezer Baptist Church read from the book of Ephesians, and the principle speaker at the dedication was Dr. Douglas S. Freeman. Following the speech, the memorial was unveiled by Mrs. H.B. Handy, the mother of Pilot Officer Richard Fuller Patterson of the Royal Canadian Force, who was killed on December 7, 1941. Within a month, vandals had defaced the memorial by marking out the names of men who had died to give those same vandals the right to live in a free land.

While Richmonders were dealing with vandals, the world was still at war. Patton's tanks were crashing through Germany, and in the Pacific, there was vicious island fighting. After crossing the sands of Iwo Jima, the United States flag was raised on the crest of Mount Suribachi. The picture of the flag-raising became iconic. Secretary of the Navy James Forrestal commented, "The raising of that flag on Suribachi means a Marine Corps for the next 500 years." And then there was the invasion of the island of Okinawa, which was accompanied by relentless kamikaze attacks on the navy ships supporting the invasion. Okinawa was needed to provide airfields close to Japan in support of air operations for the planned invasion of the Japanese home islands. Like other invasions, the United States paid a high price in casualties to capture the island.

Richmond's traditional Easter Service was held on the steps of the Capitol at 7:00 a.m. on Easter morning. The service opened with a trumpet call, and the sermon topic was "Christ, Our Hope for the Future" by Dr. J.H. Marion Jr., pastor of Grace Covenant Presbyterian Church. Thomas Jefferson High School's Glee Club sang, "The Holy City." Other services were held throughout the city. Topics included "Easter Joy in a World at War," "The Wonderful Message of Easter," "He Is Risen" and "The Eternal Quest." The *Richmond News Leader* printed a prayer in the newspaper with this petition: "Above all, we pray for our valiant fighters, for our suffering wounded, and for the bereaved among us. May their great sacrifices resurrect a lasting peace." Passover services were held in the Richmond synagogues, and a Seder for Jewish men and women in the military was held at the Hebrew Sheltering Aid Society at 215 North Nineteenth Street.

Just as December 7, 1941, will live in infamy, April 12, 1945, will live in sorrow; it was the day that President Franklin Delano Roosevelt died in Warm Springs, Georgia. Richmonders heard the news simultaneously over WRNL, WRVA and WMBG a few minutes before 6:00 p.m. (I can still remember hearing my mother cry when she heard the bulletin.) Others heard the news when it was announced in theaters, printed in the newspapers or relayed by a neighbor. By 8:25 p.m., newsboys were selling extras of the *Richmond Times-Dispatch*. Meanwhile, in Warm Springs, the president's casket was being loaded on to a train for the trip to Washington. As the casket was being carried, Graham Jackson, with tears streaming down his face, played on his accordion "Going Home," and one of the president's favorite hymns, "Nearer My God to Thee."

The *Richmond News Leader* offered the following thought: "Where else in all the annals of the presidency is there a record so amazing? How different might be the state of liberty in the world today if he had died the day of Dunkirk, instead of the day of the crossing of the Elbe." Richmonders paid their respect in many ways. Approximately 1,400 persons crowded St. Paul's Episcopal Church to honor the president at the same time as his funeral was being held at the White House. Other houses of worship held services, as did the Richmond Army Air Base and the USO. The Chinese community in Richmond attended services at the Chinese Club on West Broad Street, and the "Greek Colony" held a service at its church at 2 West Main Street. Richmond's more than 30,000 public and parochial school children also participated in memorial services held at their schools.

At the Hotel John Marshall, a dance was cancelled, as were all events at the USO. It was reported that for the first time since it opened, the USO at Second and Grace Streets was quiet. All state, city and county offices closed, as did theaters. Flags were all at half-staff, and the city hall entrance was draped in black. Many people could remember no other president, and his death was hard to accept. It left people in a state of disbelief. But there was still a war to be won, and Richmonders and the nation rallied behind their new president: Harry S Truman. President Truman had been sworn into office holding a Bible that had been found in Franklin Roosevelt's office—an office from which "Fireside Chats" had been delivered; an office where momentous decisions had been made; an office frequented by a little Scottie dog named Fala.

When Richmonders unfolded their morning newspapers on May 2, 1945, the headline read: "Hitler Dead, Germans Say." After a period of disbelief, people accepted the fact that the most hated human on the planet was dead. The German press reported that Hitler "fought until his last breath in a battle to save Berlin." (Subsequent information would reveal that he committed suicide.) One sour note appeared amid the excitement. Several local restaurants had posted signs promising free beer when Hitler was killed. When his death was announced, the signs were quickly removed, and people were irritated. Many storeowners claimed that they had not posted such signs. One store said drinks were only promised if Hitler was hanged, and he had not been hanged. Faithful to its promise, the Victory Grill on Davis Avenue served free beer, and apparently everyone had a good time. While beer was being consumed, an editorial writer was composing these words:

> *Adolf Hitler, the archfiend who brought this misery and wretchedness upon the world, apparently is dead. He or his agents murdered many of their own associates in the "blood bath" of 1934, and in subsequent years, but such crooks, thieves, liars, torturers, and homicidal maniacs as Goering, Goebbels and Himmler are as yet uncaught. We must pursue them relentlessly to the ends of the earth.*

The pursuit would not be long.

On May 7, at 9:35 a.m. EWT, there was a flash from the War Department that Germany had surrendered. The *Richmond Times-Dispatch* reported, "Unconditional surrender after nearly six years of bloodshed and destruction without parallel in all human history, brings peace to a shattered, decimated Europe." The surrender had taken place in a little red schoolhouse in Reims, France, which was the headquarters of General Eisenhower. German General Alfred Jodl signed the unconditional surrender document on behalf of Germany. Colonel James Moore Jr. of Richmond was present at the surrender. Thirty minutes after the news was broadcasted, church bells started to ring, but the celebration was rather restrained since everyone knew that the war in the Pacific was still raging, with the end still not in sight. Indeed, all Americans feared the blood bath that would surely take place when the projected invasion of the Japanese home islands began.

Of course, there were some celebrations. Some "girls made their own confetti from the little discs left by punching  machines" and tossed the homemade confetti out office windows. The corner of Grace and Fourth Streets "was white with confetti and streamers hung from the windows of office buildings." Girls at the post office on Main Street yelled at soldiers; newsboys were screaming, "Extra, extra, read all about it!"; and a florist had placed pictures of doves of peace in the store window. A sign in a photographic studio summed up the thoughts of most Richmonders. It read: "VE Day [Victory in Europe Day] Thank God."

In gratitude for the end of the war in Europe, over thirty-five thousand Richmonders attended religious services. There was a union service at

First Baptist Church. Every available spot in the church was filled, and many worshippers had to be turned away. Churchgoers sang the national anthem and "Onward Christian Soldiers," and there were also prayers for those who had died in the service of the nation. People knew the meaning of the gold star in the windows of homes where servicemen had died. Dr. Churchill Gibson of St. James Episcopal Church told of a small child who thought the evening star was God's gold star for His Son who had died. The Reverend Arthur W. Newell of St. John's Evangelical Lutheran Church offered this prayer:

> *Heavenly Father, Who hast made of one blood all nations to dwell upon the face of the earth, we bow humbly before Thee this day with hearts filled with gratitude. Should we think of rejoicing, make us conscious of the bitter suffering of our brothers in all lands and of the price with which this victory has been bought. Dedicate us to the task of building a world that shall bring liberty and justice to all. Amen.*

There were also services in Richmond's synagogues. At Sir Moses Montefiore Synagogue, the service began with the singing of "America" and the responsive reading of Psalm 92, which has the phrase: "It is a good thing to give thanks unto the Lord."

As American soldiers entered the concentration camps, they saw the emaciated bodies of the walking dead who had survived Hitler's Holocaust. The soldiers also saw piles of corpses unburied and left to rot. Master Sergeant Werner T. Angress was a Richmonder who entered the camp. He shared some of his experiences in a letter to a professor at the Richmond Professional Institute. He wrote:

> *The sight was the most horrible one I have ever seen.* [The inmates] *were all over the place; piled up, head to feet; in the latrine, in the so-called wash room; in the barrack corners. It was a repulsing sight, sickening sight. Their bodies were shrunk, only bones and skin. I don't want to tell you anymore.*

Memorial Day, the traditional start of summer was celebrated in Richmond with a parade to Hollywood Cemetery followed by the usual patriotic speeches. Graves were decorated with both United States and Confederate flags. Within a few days, it was announced that the USO Parking Lot Canteen would open every Tuesday, Thursday and Saturday night throughout the summer. Although servicemen could bring dates, there would be "hostesses ready and willing to trip the light fantastic." Shields Lake in Byrd Park was opened for swimming, but there was a concern with female bathing suits. It was reported that there would not be any sort of dress patrol on duty but that the city "will rely on the good judgment and sense of propriety of the bathers." The bare midriff suits that were designed to save cloth were quite acceptable. However, radical bathing suits would be banned. The following example was used: "Cellophane is fine for raincoats, but cellophane bathing suits would be something else again!"

July 4 was quiet in Richmond, with little celebration and few fireworks. The main sound was the splash when over seven thousand people jumped into Shields Lake, presumably with acceptable bathing suits. Other events included a celebration in Highland Park consisting of games with prizes and music by Eddie Weaver and Jim Hall and his Mountaineers.

But the freedom proclaimed on July 4, 1776, in the Declaration of Independence was still being sought by Richmond's black citizens. The newspapers still had lists of jobs where only whites need apply. As an example, the following ad appeared: "Philip Morris and Co. needs girls (white) for work in cigarette making and packing departments." There was also an uproar at the College of William and Mary when a student writer suggested that blacks be admitted and integrated into the student body. A special meeting of the Board of Visitors was called to deal with the situation, and the student newspaper was put under faculty control when publication was resumed. And the Virginia Supreme Court ruled that Virginia's racial segregation laws were valid both in intrastate and in interstate transportation. Jim Crow was still alive and well in Richmond, Virginia, although the Nazi eagle and the swastika had been blasted into oblivion.

Even though the war was still being fought against Japan, human-interest stories continued to make Richmonders laugh through their tears. A little boy took his sister's chamber pot, jammed it on his head and could not get it off. His mother took him to the Medical College of Virginia on the Lakeside bus for a pot removal. Not as humorous was the fact that grocers were making their milk supplies go further by diluting milk with water or were selling horsemeat as hamburger. Perhaps the biggest local attraction of the summer was a steeplejack who was hired to paint the flagpole on top of the Central National Bank Building. To summon the necessary courage to paint the pole, he had several drinks of gin. When his courage had been summoned, he climbed the pole, slipped and was held upside down by his safety harness for over an hour. Thousands of people kept looking at the dangling man until he was rescued by firemen and another steeplejack.

The newspaper continued to report Richmonders' roles in the war. Lieutenant Commander G.L. Street III, commanding officer of the submarine USS *Tirante* in the Pacific Ocean, made one of the most "outstanding patrols of the war" by sinking at least six Japanese ships. His citation for the Medal of Honor stated that it was awarded "for conspicuous gallantry and intrepidity at the risk of his life above and beyond the call of duty as commanding officer of the USS *Tirante* during the first war patrol of that vessel against enemy Japanese surface forces...."

The success of the USS *Tirante* was followed by the ordeal of the USS *Franklin*. In March 1945, the *Franklin* was hit by two armor-piercing bombs that turned the ship into a floating furnace. W.L. Ballard of Richmond reported that "there was a tremendous explosion and a huge sheet of flame. Things happened so fast that there was no time to be scared." Arthur Clarke of Richmond, a former photographer for the *Richmond Times-Dispatch*, was chief photographer's mate on the stricken ship and took some of the widely published pictures of the *Franklin* in flames. (Mr. Clarke also took my picture when I was graduating from high school. He told me about the pictures he took on the ship.) Although the ship was severely damaged, the *Franklin* was able to return to New York City under its own power. Constructed by the Newport News Shipbuilding and Dry Dock Company, the *Franklin* was the most heavily damaged aircraft carrier to survive the war. Casualty totals were 724 killed and 265 wounded.

While the *Franklin* was returning to a hero's welcome in New York City, B-29s were bombing Japan on an almost daily basis. One of the B-29s was named City of Richmond and was commanded by Captain Frank H. Williams Jr. of Richmond. The crew named the B-29 in honor of his hometown. In a long letter published in the newspaper, the captain wrote about one of the missions flown by the City of Richmond. He wrote, "It is hard to describe the holocaust that was already in progress in that city [Tokyo]. Smoke was billowing far above our flight altitude and the fires were spreading so rapidly it was hard to find a place to drop our incendiary bombs." Remembering his hometown, he described a Japanese city as "lit up like the Christmas tree in Capitol Square."

Starting in late July, the newspapers carried headlines almost every day about the attacks on Japan. Some of these headlines were as follows: "Jap Aircraft attacked by U.S. planes," "500 B-29s Rain Bombs on Jap Cities," "Two Jap Steel Centers Wrecked," "Fleet Close to Jap City," "US Planes pound Japan," "3 Oil Plants Hit in Raid by B-29s," "B-29s Ready to Ignite 11 Cities," "800 B-29s Blast Japan" and "Bomb Hits Enemy City with Power 2,000 Times that of Britian's Biggest." A B-29 with Enola Gay painted on its nose had dropped an atomic bomb on Hiroshima. Seeing the massive destruction, the copilot wrote, "My God, what have we done?" Japan was doomed! President Truman was emphatic when he said, "We shall completely destroy Japan's power to make war." When Japan did not surrender, a second atomic bomb was dropped on Nagasaki from the bomb bay of a B-29 named Bockscar. This attack was followed by about 100 B-29s attacking Tokyo. The fires started on December 7 at Pearl Harbor had now engulfed Japan in flames of incomprehensible retribution. Most Richmonders had no problem with the morality of dropping the atomic bomb to end the war. They still remembered Pearl Harbor.

On August 10, the newspaper reported, "This may be the day for which you have labored and prayed. If there is a delay, it will not be prolonged." Just the thought of surrender sent Richmond's officeworkers into the street. Some businesses contemplated closing to await further word of the surrender. Flags suddenly appeared on buildings. People would not leave their radios for fear of missing the news, but there was a concern that it might be a hoax, so excitement was somewhat tempered. The police reported that everyone seemed happy but with a mood of "watchful waiting." On August 12, the *Richmond Times-Dispatch* reported, "Japan Is Beaten," but the final surrender notice had not come. Then the news wires lit up.

Richmonders, listening to their radios at 7:00 p.m. Eastern War Time on August 15, 1945, heard President Harry S Truman read a statement announcing that Japan had surrendered. "Cease fire" orders were immediately flashed to the United States Pacific Fleet and to all other units under Admiral Chester Nimitz's command. World War II was over! The long fight had ended. The war that had started for Americans on that "Day of Infamy" at Pearl Harbor ended with the destruction of two Japanese cities and the capitulation of the Japanese Empire. Hearing the news, Governor Darden wrote, "By God's mercy we have escaped the incalculable disaster that has overhung Western Civilization these recent years. Thank God we are at peace again."

At the USO, servicemen heard the news of the surrender in shock, silence and disbelief. Slowly, they grasped the meaning of the president's message, and then they smiled, shook hands and started to talk. Soldiers and sailors, who seconds earlier could think only of a world at war and a return to combat, could now envision a world at peace and dared to think what it would be like when they could go home again—home to Chicago, home to New York, home to every city, town, farm and hamlet in America.

Richmond's Broad Street was virtually empty when President Truman broadcasted the news of the Japanese surrender to a waiting nation. On hearing the news, "Richmonders went wild with joy." The *Richmond Times-Dispatch* reported that "seconds after the news of Japan's surrender was flashed to the world, deserted streets in the downtown area were soon packed with people, some talking excitedly among themselves and some just staring into space as if they could not believe the end had come."

Bedlam broke loose. Cars with horns blaring streamed into downtown Richmond. At Broad and Sixth Streets, flags were waved, people smiled and V for Victory signs were flashed. Some marines screamed, "It's over! It's over!" To some pretty girls, sailors shouted, "Come on, the war is over! Let's have some fun!" Indeed, practically everyone who wanted to be kissed was accommodated on that evening.

Then the celebration got even more exciting. A fire hose was pushed through an upper-floor window at the Hotel Richmond, and passersby were sprayed with water. Not to be outdone, guests in Murphy's Hotel threw toilet paper from the windows of their rooms. The paper landed across some trolley lines, caught fire and added to the excitement. Some young people got on top of a streetcar and rode it through the city. In the midst of the chaos, newsboys were screaming, "Extra, extra, read all about it!" The paper had a two-word headline: "JAPS QUIT."

With the relief that came from knowing that the war was finally over, people started screaming, "Let's celebrate!" Whiskey bottles, some clothed by Virginia's trademark brown paper bags, were passed from mouth to mouth, while police officers looked the other way. The police also did not notice when some marines took neckties from some civilians, put them around their own necks and paraded down Broad Street. As the celebration escalated, the police had the impossible task of trying to maintain order without dampening the spirits of the assembled crowd.

Firemen, when they were not responding to false alarms, contributed to the excitement. At the fire station in the 900 block of East Broad Street, the firemen blew the sirens and rang the bells on their fire engines while other firemen gave away little American flags to all who came by. The flags, for some reason, had been stored in the firehouse since the end of the World War I. Accompanying the waving flags were cowbells. It seemed that there were plenty of cowbells, but no one knew where they came from since cows no longer lived in downtown Richmond.

In sharp contrast to the noise of the street parties was the hush of the church services. Richmond's churches opened their doors, and the faithful

A cartoon by Fred Seibel from the *Richmond Times-Dispatch*. The little crow is named Moses and appears in most of his cartoons. *Courtesy of Richmond Newspapers Incorporated.*

*Opposite*: A Richmond paper announcing the end of the war. *Author's collection.*

gave thanks for the end of the war. Father Leo J. Ryan, pastor of Sacred Heart Cathedral, "thanked God that an end had come to the years of battle and bloodshed throughout the world." The Reverend E.S. Sheppe of Boulevard Methodist Church pledged to help make "the kind of world in which our young men never again will be called upon to fight." A favorite scripture was Isaiah 2:4: "…and they shall beat their swords into plowshares, and their spears into pruning hooks: nation shall not lift up swords against nation, neither shall they learn war anymore."

The *Richmond Times-Dispatch* reminded its readers that "the joy which is felt over the Japanese surrender should be tempered by a realization that this triumph was purchased at a frightful cost." An editorial in the *Richmond News Leader* stated: "If before dawn tomorrow, some passing plane arouses you at the hour when courage is lost, you will find yourself asking still 'is my man safe?'; and you will breath your ten-thousandth prayer for him before you will realize that he is secure now from bombs and machine gun bullets!"

But amid the celebration, amid the sounds of victory and amid the prayers of the people, there were the painful memoires of those telegrams from the War Department—telegrams that notified someone that a loved one would not be coming home. More than seven hundred Richmond families received this dreaded news that opened with the words, "The War Department deeply regrets to inform you that your son/daughter was killed in action in the performance of his/her duty and in the service of his/her country. The Department extends to you its sincerest sympathy in your great loss." The end of the war ended the hope for a miracle for many families. Mr. and Mrs. W.S. Williamson of 606 North Thirty-eighth Street received a telegram that their son, Private Guy Williamson, who had been reported missing since October 22, 1944, was now reported as killed in action near Bologna, Italy. Private Williamson was the youngest songwriter in Virginia at the age of fifteen, and many of his compositions were played by Eddie Weaver. He had also been a captain in the John Marshall High School Corps of Cadets. One can only speculate about how many other men and women who died in the war, regardless of the uniform they wore, could have contributed to the betterment of society.

September 2, 1945, was VJ Day (Victory over Japan Day). Jack Stone of WRVA Radio was on board the battleship USS *Missouri* anchored in Tokyo Bay, under a cloudy sky, waiting for the Japanese delegation to arrive and sign the surrender documents. He was the only correspondent from a Virginia radio station on board. Flying from the *Missouri*'s flagstaff was the same flag that was flying over the nation's capitol on the "Day of Infamy." The Japanese delegation signed the instruments of surrender that had been placed on a mess hall table covered with a green coffee-stained tablecloth. Thus ended the war that had lasted 1,364 days, 5 hours and 44 minutes. The surrender proceedings lasted only 23 minutes. The ceremony was cold and formal, with no handshakes, surrender of swords or any other of the traditional ceremonies associated with capitulation. Speaking for the United States, General Douglas MacArthur said, "Let us pray that peace be now restored to the world and that God will preserve it always." As the ceremonies concluded, 450 planes from the nearby aircraft carriers screamed over the *Missouri* at masthead height as the sun broke through the clouds.

Richmonders were proud to hear that the USS *Richmond*, a light cruiser, participated in the occupation of northern Japan. From the White House, President Truman promised, "We shall not forget Pearl Harbor." Richmonders soon realized that life was getting back to normal. Parking meters were put back in place, speed limits were raised to fifty-five miles per hour, long-delayed vacations were planned, gas and oil rationing ended, war surplus foxhole shovels were available for ninety-eight cents at Kaufman's, returning servicemen were looking for jobs, some women continued to work, students started back to school, store clerks began being courteous again and a bus waited for an elderly Negro woman to board it. The woman thanked the driver, and she responded with: "You're welcome."

Japanese surrender on board the USS *Missouri* that ended World War II. *National Archives.*

Memories of World War II still linger in Richmond today. Cemeteries are filled with those who gave their "last full measure of devotion." The Belgium Building, where so many men were inducted into military service, still stands on the campus of Virginia Union University. The building used by the Patent Office is still standing on Lombardy Street, as are many of the churches and synagogues where people prayed for those across the seas.

The former Central National Bank Building, where the mayor of Richmond observed the blackouts, still towers over the nearby buildings. The memorial in Monroe Park still stands but has largely been forgotten. Outside the Cathedral of the Sacred Heart there is a statue to the Jewish victims of Hitler's hate. On it is inscribed, "Rachel weeping for her children." The Virginia War Memorial overlooks Lee Bridge, where soldiers once stood guard and over which convoys headed for various military camps. To stand in the memorial is to stand in a hallowed place where the wandering spirits of those who died for freedom can still be felt.

Many years have passed since Richmonders lived through the ordeal of World War II, and although the memories of those tragic days have faded, they must never be forgotten. The sacrifices of those who died on bloody

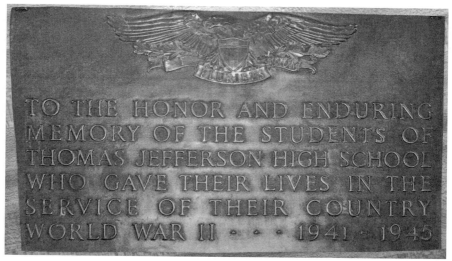

The plaque at Thomas Jefferson High School in memory of those who died in World War II. *Author's collection.*

*Top*: Virginia War Memorial, Richmond, Virginia. *Photograph by Walter Griggs.*

*Opposite, top*: The United States Patent Office in World War II. It is now a U-Haul facility. *Photograph by Walter Griggs.*

*Opposite, bottom*: U.S. Highway 1—the route of many convoys during the war. It is now a Blue Star Memorial Highway. *Photograph by Walter Griggs.*

The National Cemetery on Williamsburg Road, Memorial Day 2013. *Photograph by Cara F. Griggs.*

battlefields, sailed through hostile waters, flew through flax-filled skies, served as air-raid wardens, worked in factories or smashed tin cans flat must always be remembered. Although the gold stars are gone from windows, the stars in the heavens still shine on this land of the "free and the home of the brave."

When the Carillon was dedicated shortly before the outbreak of Hitler's rise to power in Europe, the bells rang out "America." As the war ended, there was another concert where the same bells rang out the music to the same words:

> *My country, 'tis of thee*
> *Sweet land of liberty,*
> *Of thee I sing;*
> *Land where my fathers died,*
> *Land of the pilgrims' pride*
> *From ev'ry mountainside*
> *Let freedom ring!*

# BIBLIOGRAPHY

## BOOKS

Dabney, Virginius. *Richmond: The Story of a City*. Charlottesville: University of Virginia Press, 1990.

Fosdick, Harry Emerson. *A Great Time to Be Alive*. New York: Harper and Row, 1944.

Goodman, Jack. *While You Were Away*. New York: Simon and Schuster, 1946.

Hoehling, A.A. *Home Front U.S.A.* New York: Thomas Y. Crowell Company, 1966.

Lutz, Francis. *Richmond in World War II*. Richmond, VA: Dietz Press, Inc., 1951.

Schlegel, Marvin Wilson. *Virginia on Guard*. Richmond: Virginia State Library, 1949.

## ARTICLES

Martin, Pete. "Tredegar Iron Works." *Saturday Evening Post*, July 24, 1943.

## NEWSPAPERS

*Norfolk Ledger-Dispatch*, June 1–30, 1940.

*Richmond Afro-American*, January 1, 1942–December 25, 1945.

*Richmond News Leader*, November 1, 1937–December 25, 1945.

*Richmond Times-Dispatch*, November 1, 1937–December 25, 1945.

# ABOUT THE AUTHOR

D r. Walter S. Griggs Jr. is a professor at Virginia Commonwealth University in Richmond, Virginia, where he teaches law. He has also taught history courses in the Honors College. He holds a master's degree from the University of Richmond, a juris doctorate from the University of Richmond School of Law and a doctorate from the College of William and Mary in Virginia. Griggs has written books on the Church Hill

*Photo by Cara F. Griggs.*

Tunnel and *The Hidden History of Richmond* (both published by The History Press), the Civil War and moose, as well as numerous academic articles. He was awarded the Jefferson Davis Medal for his Civil War articles and books. Griggs is married to the former Frances Pitchford, who, fortunately, is a retired English teacher. She edits and proofs his work. He is equally fortunate to have a daughter, Cara, who is an archivist for the Library of Virginia. Walter Griggs and his family live in Richmond.